Promoting
The Common Good

Bringing Economics and Theology
Together Again

Promoting
The Common Good

Bringing Economics and Theology
Together Again

KAMRAN MOFID

AND

MARCUS BRAYBROOKE

SHEPHEARD-WALWYN (PUBLISHERS) LTD

First published in 2005 by
Shepheard-Walwyn (Publishers) Ltd
Suite 604, The Chandlery
50 Westminster Bridge Road
London SE1 7QY

British Library Cataloguing in Publication Data
A catalogue record of this book
is available from the British Library

ISBN 0 85683 231 6

Typeset by Alacrity
Banwell Castle, Weston-super-Mare
Printed by English Press Ltd, Nairobi, Kenya

Sooner or later, all the peoples of the world will have to discover a way to live together in peace, and thereby transform this pending cosmic elegy into a creative psalm of brotherhood. If this is to be achieved, man must evolve for all human conflict a method which rejects revenge, aggression, and retaliation. The foundation of such a method is love.

REV DR MARTIN LUTHER KING, JR

'With what shall I come before the Lord, and bow myself before God on high? Shall I come before him with burnt offerings, with calves a year old? Will the Lord be pleased with thousands of rams, with ten thousands of rivers of oil? Shall I give my firstborn for my transgression, the fruit of my body for the sin of my soul?' He has told you, O mortal, what is good; and what does the Lord require of you but to do justice, and to love kindness, and to walk humbly with your God?

PROPHET MICAH

Now is the Time

Now is the time to know
That all that you do is sacred.

Now, why not consider
A lasting truce with yourself and God?
Now is the time for the world to know
That every thought and action is sacred.

This is the time for you to compute the impossibility
That there is anything
But Grace.

Now is the season to know
That everything you do
Is sacred.

HAFEZ

Ultimately, we have just one moral duty: to reclaim large areas of peace in ourselves, more and more peace, and to reflect it towards others. And the more peace there is in us, the more peace there will be in our troubled world.

ETTY HILLESUM

This book is dedicated to all of those who have inspired us

Contents

Acknowledgements

MARCUS BRAYBROOKE and I, in preparing this project, have benefited greatly from our association with many inspiring people across the world. To all those mentioned in this book, and to many others whom space alone has kept us from naming, we would like to extend grateful thanks. We dedicate this book to all of those who have inspired us.

We are particularly grateful to Richard Harries, Bishop of Oxford, and Bhai Sahib Mohinder Singh, Chairman and Spiritual Successor of the Guru Nanak Nishkam Sewak Jatha in Birmingham, England, for respectively writing the Foreword and Epilogue to our book. With their support and endorsement, this study is much richer and more fulfilling than it would otherwise have been.

In the production of this book, we are grateful to our publisher, Anthony Werner at Shepheard-Walwyn, for his moral, spiritual and academic support. Likewise, we extend very warm appreciation to Jean Desebrock at Alacrity for her excellent work and personal support in preparing the manuscript for publication. We are also most thankful to the audiovisual team, especially Nirmal and Sukhi, at Guru Nanak Nishkam Sewak Jatha, for their excellent work in designing and producing the book jacket. We are also grateful to Harjinder S. Panesar, Director of Pressmaster Ltd, and Kalpan Patel, Director of the English Press Ltd in Nairobi, Kenya, for their helpful assistance in the printing of the book.

Our wives, Mary and Annie, have been a constant source of support and joy. Their deep commitment to faith and economic justice have given us the inspiration to do what we do. For that we are grateful to them. Their daily care for us, and the love of our children, reminds us never to take lightly the issues explored in this book.

Any failure on the part of the reader to comprehend our arguments will be due completely to our own shortcomings and not to our sources of inspiration: they are not culpable for any inadequacy in our attempts to formulate a faithful response to the question of how to relate theology and economics.

In my chapters I have attempted to present my thoughts in an easy-to-read manner and so have opted to give references to sources consulted at the end of the book, to spare the reader from being distracted by excessive annotation. In this way I hope to carry the reader more closely with me, so that we may have a fruitful dialogue; it is one of the main objects of this study.

KAMRAN MOFID

Foreword

BY RICHARD HARRIES, BISHOP OF OXFORD

THERE WAS A TIME when economics was regarded as a branch of theology. Economic factors were intimately linked to what was regarded as just or right and these in their turn were shaped by a Christian understanding of the common good. From the eighteenth century onwards economics became an autonomous discipline and this has clearly enabled a great deal of technical expertise to be developed. Nevertheless in the end economics is about human well-being in society and this cannot be separated from moral, or perhaps in the end, theological considerations. The idea of an economics which is value-free is totally spurious. Nothing in this life is morally neutral. Although of course there will continue to be a range of technical, very often statistical and mathematical factors in economics, in the end the subject cannot be separated from a vision of what it is to be a human being in society.

Globalisation has sharply divided people today. On the one hand there are anti-capitalist, anti-globalisation campaigners and on the other hand those who believe that the process of globalisation will solve the world's economic ills. Both these positions are false. Whether we like it or not globalisation is taking place and will continue to accelerate. The question is whether the forces at work in the process can be harnessed and made to work for the well-being of human society as a whole.

I very much welcome this book and believe that its themes are of crucial importance for the world today.

Abstract

BY KAMRAN MOFID

THE TOPIC which we wish to address here is vast; all we can reasonably hope to do is paint a picture with very broad brushstrokes. We will argue that the marketplace is not just an an economic sphere, 'it is a region of the human spirit'. The secrets of a great many economic questions are divine in nature; economics should (in contrast to the way it is practised today) be concerned with the world of the heart and spirit. Although self-interest is an important source of human motivation, driving the decisions we make in the marketplace every day, those decisions nevertheless have a moral, ethical and spiritual content, because each decision we make affects not only ourselves but others too.

Today's economists consider their discipline a science, and thus divorced from inconvenient ethical details, the normative passions of right and wrong. They have made their discipline a moral-free zone. Yet the role of virtue in economics had been extolled since Aristotle. Adam Smith, in the eighteenth century, called human society an 'immense machine', and celebrated virtue as the 'fine polish' on its wheels. He excoriated vice as the 'rust' that causes the wheels to 'jar and grate upon one another'. Ethical considerations are central to life, he said, and 'keen and earnest attention to the propriety of our own conduct ... constitutes the real essence of virtue'. Modern economics began as a moral science taught by professors trained in the analysis of ethical contexts and conflicts. Smith's *The Wealth of Nations* (1776) is both a scientific treatise on economic development and a forceful statement about the ethics of markets and distribution of income. Justice is central to his analysis and recommendations. When he elaborates on how global markets can yield greater efficiency, the issue of 'justice' arises about once every seven pages. In his earlier work, *The Theory of Moral Sentiments* (1759), Smith depicts justice as a moral concept of right and wrong that goes beyond legality. To him, 'Justice ... is the main pillar that upholds the whole edifice. If it is removed, the great, the immense fabric of human society ... must in a moment crumble into atoms.' He accordingly creates a model which allows for the development of moral conscience, and social capital in the form of trust and personal responsibility. This is the now dismissed ethical framework for his famous 'invisible hand'. That oversight is where modern neo-liberal economics has got it so wrong, bringing the world such a bitter harvest.

This study views the problem and challenge of globalisation partly from economic but primarily from ethical, spiritual and theological points of view. How can we order the modern world so that we may all live well and live in peace? Globalisation must combine economic efficiency with human needs to achieve social justice and a sustainable environment.

We moreover argue for the creation of an 'ecumenical space' for dialogue between civilisations, and for the building of community for the common good, by bringing together economics, spirituality and theology.

CHAPTER 1

Globalisation
for the Common Good

BY KAMRAN MOFID

TODAY THE GLOBALISED world economy, despite many significant achievements during the last few decades, and especially since the end of the Second World War in areas such as science, technology, medicine, transport and communication, is facing major, potentially catastrophic, socio-economic, political, cultural and environmental crises.

We are surrounded by global problems of inequality, injustice, poverty, greed, marginalisation, exclusion, intolerance, fear, mistrust, xenophobia, terrorism, sleaze and corruption. These problems are affecting the overall fabric of societies in many parts of the world.

The twentieth century was the bloodiest in human history, with holocausts, genocides, ethnic cleansing, two world wars and hundreds of intra- and international wars. After decades of selfishness, greed, individualism and emphasis on wealth-creation without care about how this wealth is being created, the world is today entering a period of reflection and self-examination, and perhaps a spiritual revolution.

Many people around the globe have come to the conclusion that it would be possible to create a better world if only a critical mass of people, with a sense of decency and a belief in the ultimate goodness of humanity, would rise up and realise their power to transform the world. More and more people around the world are starting to see that there are no short cuts to happiness. Material wealth is important – this should not be denied – but it is only one ingredient of happiness. A complete sense of inner peace and tranquillity can be achieved only through basing one's actions on virtues such as wisdom, justice, ethics, love and humanity. This spiritual revolution needs architecture and dedicated architects.

Today's financial globalisation, of which we hear so much, has created an environment and culture in which individual self-interest takes priority over social good. A transactional view of the world dominates economic thinking; personal relationships and the creation of a stable society are largely ignored in the maximisation of profits. Economic globalisation without compassion and concern for the common good creates a house of cards, ready to be blown away by forces it ultimately would not be able to control. The historian Arnold Toynbee, who traced the rise and fall of civilisations, asserted that spirituality was more significant than political leaders in the rise of civilisations, and that once a civilisation lost its spiritual core it sank into decline. This should be a lesson to those who believe they can create and control civilisations through brutal force.

In 2002 my book *Globalisation for the Common Good* was published, and the following year my booklet, *Business Ethics, Corporate Social Responsibility and Globalisation for the Common Good*. My main aim in both was to provide a critique of modern economics and the way it is taught in our universities around the world. I tried to use jargon-free language that was accessible to the general reader. Economics greatly influences public policy all over the world and, having trained as an economist and having taught it in universities for over two decades, I felt I should share its shortcomings with those most affected by it, namely the general public, including my students.

My secondary objective was to outline how economics could be developed to show a better understanding of how the world really works, of what this life is really all about, instead of simplistically encouraging us to produce and consume more and more every day. I wanted to teach my students a different economics. I wanted to be able to engage with them on the bigger questions: how could our economic models and theories help us order the world so that we may all live well and live in peace and happiness?

This current study summarises my thinking over the past few years, and especially since the publication of *Globalisation for the Common Good*. Again it is simply written: it aims to be my dialogue with members of the general public. It is the fruit of my engagement with many people from different walks of life and from many different parts of the world. I have learnt a great deal from them, and I have been much inspired by them.

After teaching modern neo-classical economics for over twenty years, I had begun to see the light. I knew that I was going through a process of major personal rediscovery, although I was not yet sure where I was going.

In my previous publications I argued for a compassionate economics, explaining that the world needs a new vision of peace rooted in justice. We need a united international community dedicated to the well-being of all humanity and all creation. I explained why we need to bring together economics, compassion, love and justice in order to create a 'globalisation for the common good'.

However, I had not yet shared with my readers the personal motivation behind these ideals. What had happened to me that changed me so profoundly? Now I would like to share my personal journey with the reader. It has been an intellectual, emotional and spiritual journey; it has involved wrestling with a diverse range of concepts, ideas concerning the relationship between economics, theology and spirituality as well as concerns for human dignity and socio-economic justice.

I hope that my journey will inspire others, especially fellow economists, and particularly the younger generation, to strive whole-heartedly and all the way for what they believe to be right and just. They have a very important mission and a difficult journey ahead of them. Edward Fullbrook in *A Guide to What's Wrong with Economics* describes what they are up against:

From the 1960s onward, neoclassical economists have increasingly managed to block the employment of non-neoclassical economists, narrow the economics curriculum offered by universities to students, and make their theories increasingly irrelevant to understanding economic reality. Now, they are even banishing economic history and the history of economic thought from the curriculum.

I sincerely hope that my experiences, which I will describe to you in my next chapter, will not be shared by any of the new generation of economists. A few years back, when I started to be a 'non-orthodox' economist asking awkward questions, I felt isolated and rejected, not knowing whether there were others in my field, however small in number, who felt as I did. Through *Globalisation for the Common Good* I discovered a few of them; since then I have made more discoveries – but the number is still too small. Hopefully in the future more will find the courage to discuss what is rotten in the house of neo-liberal economics.

In Chapter 2 I will be explaining how and why my idea for *Globalisation for the Common Good* developed. Chapter 4 will shed light on the roots of economics and provide a brief analysis of the way in which modern economics has gone so badly wrong. Chapter 6 will be a discussion of why religion-based economics matter. I will explore the reasons why economic analysis has, more and more over recent decades, become detached from morality and spirituality. I will discuss the implications of this segmentation for the discipline of economics and all those affected by its dictates. Finally, in Chapter 8, I will offer my recommendations for the synthesis of economics and theology.

CHAPTER 2

The Story of My Life

I was ready to tell
the story of my life
but the ripple of tears
and the agony of my heart
wouldn't let me.

I began to stutter,
saying a word here and there,
and all along I felt
as tender as a crystal
ready to be shattered

in this stormy sea
we call life.
All the big ships
come apart
board by board,

how can I survive
riding a lonely
little boat
with no oars
and no arms?

My boat was finally broken
by the waves
and I broke free
as I tied myself
to a single board.

Though the panic is gone,
I am now offended –

why should I be so helpless,
rising with one wave
and falling with the next?

I don't know
if I am
non-existence
while I exist
but I know for sure
when I am
I am not
but
when I am not
then I am.

Now how can I be
a sceptic
about the
resurrection and
coming to life again

since in this world
I have many times
like my own imagination
died and
been born again?

That is why,
after a long agonising life
as a hunter,
I finally let go and got
hunted down and became free

RUMI

CHAPTER 2

How It All Began

BY KAMRAN MOFID

I WAS BORN in Tehran, Iran in 1952. In 1971, after finishing high school, I came to England to further my education. In 1974 I married my English wife, Annie, and two years later we emigrated to Canada. I received my BA and MA in Economics from the University of Windsor in 1980 and 1982 respectively. We returned to England in 1982, and in 1986 I was awarded my PhD in Economics from the University of Birmingham.

From 1980 onwards, for the next twenty years, I taught economics in universities, enthusiastically demonstrating how economic theories provided answers to problems of all sorts. I got quite carried away by the beauty, the sophisticated elegance, of complicated mathematical models and theories. But gradually I started to have an empty feeling. I began to suspect that neo-liberal economics was an emperor with no clothes. What good were elegant theories which were unable to explain all the poverty, exclusion, racism, corruption, injustice and unhappiness that exist in the world?

Like a fellow enlightened economist, Muhammad Yunus, I came to feel that my life as a lecturer was like a make-believe movie: sit and relax … in the end models dreamt up by detached economists will sort out the world's ills! My classrooms were becoming unreal places. I began to ask fundamental questions of myself. Why did I never talk to my students about compassion, dignity, comradeship, solidarity, happiness, spirituality – about the meaning of life? We never debated the biggest questions. Who am I? Where have I come from? Where am I going to?

I told them to create wealth, but I did not tell them for what reason. I told them about scarcity and competition, but not about abundance and co-operation. I told them about free trade, but not about fair trade; about GNP – Gross National Product – but not about GNH – Gross National Happiness. I told them about profit maximisation and cost minimisation, about the highest returns to the shareholders, but not about social consciousness, account-ability to the community, sustainability and respect for creation and the creator. I did not tell them that, without humanity, economics is a house of cards built on shifting sands. Where was the economic theory that reflected my students' real lives? How could I carry on believing in such an unreal world? I could not go on asking them to believe unbelievable theories in the name of economics.

I wanted to run away from all the white elephants: the barren theories and models in my textbooks, the depart-ment of economics, the MBA programme which created managers who couldn't manage anything. I could not carry on defending the indefensible. How could I respect mod-ern economics when it had no respect for other disciplines?

These conflicts caused me much frustration and alien-ation, leading to heartache and despair. I needed to redis-cover myself and a real-life economics. After a proud twenty-year academic career, I resigned from my position as lecturer and, after a debilitating year of soul-searching, decided that I would become a student all over again. I would study theology and philosophy, disciplines nobody had taught me when I was a student of economics.

It was at this difficult time that I came to understand that I needed to bring spirituality, compassion, ethics and morality back into economics itself, to make this dismal science once again relevant to and concerned with the common good. It was now that I made the following discoveries:

• Economics, from the time of Plato right through to Adam Smith and John Stuart Mill, was as deeply concerned with issues of social justice, ethics and morality as it was with economic analysis. Most economics students today learn that Adam Smith was the 'father of modern economics' but not that he was also a moral philosopher. In 1759, sixteen years before his famous *Wealth of Nations*, he published *The Theory of Moral Sentiments*, which explored the self-interested nature of man and his ability nevertheless to make moral decisions based on factors other than selfishness. In *The Wealth of Nations*, Smith laid the early groundwork for economic analysis, but he embedded it in a broader discussion of social justice and the role of government. Students today know only of his analogy of the 'invisible hand' and refer to him as defending free markets. They ignore his insight that the pursuit of wealth should not take precedence over social and moral obligations, and his belief that a 'divine Being' gives us 'the greatest quantity of happiness'. They are taught that the free market as a 'way of life' appealed to Adam Smith but not that he distrusted the morality of the market as a morality for society at large. He neither envisioned nor prescribed a capitalist society, but rather a 'capitalist economy within society, a society held together by communities of non-capitalist and non-market morality'. That morality for Smith included neighbourly love, an obligation to practice justice, a norm of financial support for the government 'in proportion to [one's] revenue', and a tendency in human nature to derive pleasure from the good fortune and happiness of other people.

• The leading figure in the establishment of the American Economic Association (AEA) in 1885 was the progressive economist Richard T. Ely. He sought to combine economic theory with Christian ethics, especially the command to love one's neighbour (as did Adam Smith). He declared that the Church, the State and the individual must work together to fulfil the Kingdom of God on earth. Few economists or economics students today know much of this history: that, for example, twenty of the fifty founding members of the AEA were former or practising ministers. Ely himself was a leading member, in the 1880s, of the Social Gospel movement; he was better know to the American public in this capacity than as an economist. He believed that economics departments should be located in schools of theology because 'Christianity is primarily concerned with this world, and it is the mission of Christianity to bring to pass here a kingdom of righteousness.' As a 'religious subject', economics should provide the base for 'a never-ceasing attack on every wrong institution, until the earth becomes a new earth, and all its cities, cities of God.'

• The focus of economics should be on the benefit and the bounty that the economy produces, on how to let this bounty increase, and how to share the benefits justly among the people for the common good, removing the evils that hinder this process.

• 'Economic rationality' in the shape of neo-liberal globalisation is socially and politically suicidal. Justice and democracy are sacrificed on the altar of a mythical market as forces outside society rather than creations of it.

• Every apparently economic choice is, in reality, a social choice. We can choose a society of basic rights – education, health, housing, child support and a dignified pension – or greed, pandemic inequality, ecological vandalism, civic chaos and social despair. Modern neo-liberal economics ignores the first and promotes the second path as the way to achieve economic efficiency and growth.

• The moral crises of global economic injustice today are integrally spiritual: they signal something terribly amiss in the relationship between human beings and God.

• Where the moral life and the mystery of God's presence are held in one breath – because the moral life is the same as the mystical life – the moral agency may be found for establishing paths towards a more just, compassionate and sustainable way of living. 'Moral agency' is the active love of creation (for oneself as well as for other people and for the non-human creation); it is the will to orient life around the ongoing well-being of communities and of the global community, prioritising the needs of the most vulnerable; it is the will to create social structures and policies that ensure social justice and ecological sustainability.

• In contrast to this sensibility, which weds spirituality and morality, stands modern economics' persistent tendency to divorce the two, in particular to dissociate the intimate personal experience of a close relationship with God from public moral power.

• It is the belief in collective responsibility and collective endeavour that allows individual freedom to flourish. This can only be realised when we commit ourselves to the common good and begin to serve it.

• There are three justifications for the common good which are not commonly discussed in economics:

1 Human beings need human contact, or sociability. The quality of that interaction is important, quite apart from any material benefits it may bring.

2 Human beings are formed in the community – their education and training in virtue (their preferences) are elements of the common good.

3 A healthy love for the common good is a necessary component of a fully developed personality.

• The marketplace is not just an economic sphere, 'it is a region of the human spirit'. Profound economic questions

are divine in nature; in contrast to what is assumed today,
they should be concerned with the world of the heart and
spirit. Although self-interest is an important source of
human motivation, driving the decisions we make in the
marketplace every day, those decisions nevertheless have a
moral, ethical and spiritual content, because each decision
we make affects not only ourselves but others too. We must
combine the need for economic efficiency with the need for
social justice and environmental sustainability.

• The greatest achievement of modern globalisation will
eventually come to be seen as the opening up of possibil-
ities to build a humane and spiritually enriched globalised
world through the universalising and globalising of compassion. But for 'others' to become 'us', for the world to
become intimate with itself, we have to get to know each
other better than we do now. Prejudices have to disappear:
we have to see that the cultural, religious and ethnic differences reflect an ultimate creative principle. For this to
happen, the great cultures and religions need to enter into
genuine dialogue with each other.

• Finally, today more than ever before, given the collapse
of Communism and the increasing human and environmental cost of capitalism, there is a pressing need for
alternative economic models. Activists are renewing
Martin Buber's search for what in 1943 he called 'a
genuine third alternative ... leading beyond individualism
and collectivism, for the life decision of future generations'.
Crises for our species such as mass starvation, Aids, unre-
strained violence and the degradation of our biosphere –
crises that transcend economic systems, political dogmas
and national boundaries – are bringing us face-to-face with
questions about self-preservation and self-restraint, personal and communal responsibility, moral authority and
political power – questions that are at the very core of our
religious traditions. If the idea of divine authority offends

contemporary sensibilities, the environmental imperatives of creation may be seen to be as pressing as any divine commandments. The 'market value' of the world's great faiths is at an all-time high in the ongoing enterprise of human liberation. It is time to call for a theological economics which can bring us sustainability for the common good.

After concluding my theological studies, I wrote a number of books and articles on my newly discovered areas of interest and founded an annual international conference, 'An Interfaith Perspective on Globalisation for the Common Good', to address the problems and challenges of globalisation not only from an economic perspective but also from ethical, moral, spiritual and theological points of view.

My first conference ('Common Goals, Common Crises, Common Call and Common Hope') was held in Oxford in 2002. I did not know what to expect, or how many would turn up, but I was convinced it was the right thing to do. We succeeded beyond my wildest dreams. We had sixty senior speakers and many other participants from different parts of the world. I felt humbled and honoured. It was during this Oxford conference that I was pressed by many delegates to make it an annual event.

I enthusiastically took up the challenge but decided that, as we were concerned with globalisation, the conference should be held in a different country each year, extending the opportunities for dialogue and of learning from each other. Moreover, each conference was to be in association with a local organisation with aims similar to ours. So our first conference in Oxford gave birth to a global movement to promote and serve the common good.

The second conference, 'Ethics, Spirituality and Religions: Transforming Globalisation for the Common Good', was held in St Petersburg in 2003, co-convened with Dr Tatiana Roskoshnaya, Director of the Institute for Ecological Security in St Petersburg. I had previously met Tatiana in London while attending a conference and she had shared with me her concern for what was taking place in Russia under the name of free-market privatisation and deregulation. She invited us to hold the conference there, believing it could demonstrate that there are alternatives to the economics of individualism and greed. Once again it was very successful, with forty-four senior speakers and many other international participants.

The third conference, 'Integrity, Spirituality, Ethics and Accountability: Transforming Business, Corporate Social Responsibility and Globalisation for the Common Good' was held in Dubai in 2004, again with forty-four senior speakers and many other participants. We were truly grateful to the Iranian Business Council (IBC) in Dubai for organising a wonderful event, 'Iran and Globalisation for the Common Good', followed by an unforgettable Persian Gala Dinner and entertainment. The event was under the Patronage of HH Sheikh Hamdan Bin Rashid Al Maktoum, Deputy Ruler of Dubai and Minster of Finance. Six hundred invited guests, senior politicians and businessmen, foreign diplomats, academics and religious and cultural leaders, attended the event. Thanks to IBC and its visionary President Abbas Bolurfrushan we were able to share our vision with some of the most senior global leaders.

The fourth conference, 'Africa and Globalisation for the Common Good: The Quest for Justice and Peace' will be held at the Nishkam Puran Institute (NPI) in Kericho, Kenya, in April 2005 under the esteemed patronage of the Hon Dr A.A. Moody Awori, MP, Kenyan Vice-President and Minister for Home Affairs. It will be co-convened with Bhai Sahib Mohinder Singh, known to all as Baba Ji, whom I had the pleasure of meeting at our first conference in Oxford. I owe a special word of thanks and gratitude to Baba Ji for his kind support and blessings for our work, without which I could not have progressed so far or so efficiently. He is a kind and supportive friend to many. He is also a visionary religious leader, under whose chairmanship the Guru Nanak Nishkam Sewak Jatha has contributed so greatly to interfaith understanding, dialogue amongst civilisations and a more harmonious world. I am most grateful to Baba Ji and the Sikh community, in particular to those in Birmingham and Kenya, for the love and support they have given me. Baba Ji has demonstrated the power of religions to do good when truly united in spirituality, love and compassion.

The fifth conference, to be held at the Chaminade University of Honolulu in 2006 as part of a series of events celebrating the fiftieth anniversary of the university, will be co-convened with a long-term friend of globalisation for the common good, Professor David Coleman.

Our work has benefited greatly from the opening of our own website (www.commongood.info), for which I am grateful to my good friend and colleague Dr Josef Boehle.

CHAPTER 3

A Map of My Interfaith Journey

BY MARCUS BRAYBROOKE

JUST OVER forty years ago, I climbed on board an Air
India Boeing on the way to a year's study at Madras
Christian College. It was a journey that was to provide
a map for my interfaith journey.

In preparing for ordination, I had already become inter-
ested in the relationship of Christianity to other religions,
although there was little chance at that time to learn about
this as part of the Cambridge theology tripos. In India, I
could learn first-hand about several religions. At Madras
Christian College I studied under a Hindu professor who
introduced me to the teaching of Sri Ramakrishna, and to
the mystical tradition in Christianity as well as in Hinduism. I also attended seminars at Madras University. My
professor arranged for me to stay with a number of his
Brahmin friends, which gave me the chance to travel and
to see how high caste Hindus were adapting their lifestyle
to a changing society. I also had some chance to meet
Muslims and some Sikhs, and I visited Fr Murray Roger's
beautiful ashram at Joyotiniketan, where I learned about
the spiritual meeting of people of different faiths 'in the
cave of the heart'. On my return, after a year at Wells Theological College, I was invited to be a curate at Highgate in
London, where my vicar allowed me to study part-time
under Professor Geoffrey Parrinder at London University.
I first met him when he gave a lecture to the World
Congress of Faiths (WCF), of which I became a member
and soon Honorary Secretary. My particular responsibility

17

was to arrange the annual conference, which put me in contact with a wide range of creative and original religious thinkers. This was at a time when the growing number of immigrants, many from the Indian sub-continent, was prompting the Church and the government to begin to think about the implications of having sizeable communities of other faiths living in Britain. I got involved in efforts to change the pattern of Religious Instruction, as it was then known, and in discussions about whether members of other faiths could use Christian buildings for their worship. The WCF's Annual All Faiths Services were the most controversial activity.

If India introduced me to a world of many religions, there was no escape there from the grim poverty, which drains people of their human dignity – although I had seen a little of this during my National Service in North Africa. During the year in India, I was invited by a Methodist pastor, whose son was at the college, to spend Christmas in a remote village in Andhra Pradesh. I saw the crippling effect of the caste system and the degradation of the outcastes, or *dalits* as they are now known. Some of the students at Madras Christian College helped at a clinic for people suffering from leprosy. We set out by bus in the middle of the day and then walked some distance to the clinic. On the way we passed a compound where a 'criminal' tribe had been settled. The women, in the blazing sun, were breaking up, with small hammers, stones which would be used to repair the roads – work which robbed them of their human dignity. The clinic itself was a sign of hope – the children's liveliness was catching (leprosy, despite my initial fears, wasn't!) Sometimes I would go to the clinic with a Christian student from Sri Lanka and a Muslim student. The doctor was a devout Hindu. Here were people of different faiths working together for the common good, to relieve human suffering. That has remained my inspiration in all the interfaith work in which I have been engaged – the coming together of people of faith for the common good.

This awareness of the depth of human need made me restless with the curriculum and preoccupations of a theological college. The greatest blessing of that time was my marriage to Mary, who was a Methodist and a social worker. An ecumenical marriage then was almost as difficult as an interfaith marriage today – I don't mean in terms of our relationship but in terms of the attitudes of family and church dignitaries! A year in the 'united' Church of South India had already made me impatient with denominational differences.

My concerns for Christian unity and for the needs of the poor have been priorities for me during my ministry. When I became a curate in Highgate, I helped to form a Council of Churches and I organised a Christian Aid Committee (in the sixties Christian Aid was still quite new). When we moved to the Medway Towns I became chair of the Christian Aid committee in that area. Every year, at the beginning of May, an enormous lorry would draw up outside our house to deliver some seventy thousand Christian Aid envelopes and leaflets, which then had to be sent to all the churches in the area. I also helped to start an Action for World Development Group, which soon became part of the Word Development Movement.

Most of my ministry has been based in a parish, and for me rootedness in a faith community is a necessary concomitant of interfaith encounter. But interfaith work has been my 'hobby' (it has always been a voluntary unpaid activity). This work has many dimensions, but I have always hoped that the coming together of people of faith was not just a religious preoccupation but an essential for the common good. Great efforts have been made to remove ignorance and prejudice – not least in the relationship between Christians and Jews – but it is a continuing task, especially today in promoting a true appreciation of Islam. Some of my books are intended to help Christians have a better understanding of members of other religions and to discover their spiritual treasures. Even more important in dispelling prejudice is meeting with members of another faith – so organising lectures, conferences and tours has helped to build a fellowship of faiths. It has also been necessary to address theological issues. Religious exclusivism and claims to uniqueness often inhibit open dialogue and co-operation. My own belief is that the more deeply committed we are to our own faith, the greater our reverence for the faith of other people. By sharing our convictions, each of us grows in our appreciation of the Divine Mystery.

The above are absorbing and enriching concerns. Increasingly, however, amongst those engaged in interfaith activity, there is a deep and trusting enough relationship to work together for the common good. Often this will be in the form of relief activity, working for peace and reconciliation or campaigning for the environment. But I believe the faiths have an even more fundamental task, which is to question the values which are dominant in our world today and to call people to a way of life which is non-violent and self-giving.

To achieve this, it is I believe necessary for the international interfaith organisations to work together more closely, and for some twenty years I have played a part in encouraging this. In the mid-eighties, the World Congress of Faiths convened a meeting of representatives of international interfaith organisations at Ammerdown, near Bath in England. From this grew a commitment of four leading organisations – the International Association for Religious Freedom, the Temple of Understanding, the World Conference on Religion and Peace and the World Congress of Faiths – to mark the centenary of the World Parliament of Religions, which was held in Chicago in 1893, as a 'Year of Inter-religious Understanding and Co-operation'. These organisations also joined together to arrange an international conference, known as 'Sarva-Dharma-Sammelana', which was held at Bangalore in 1993. This was a gathering of people actively committed to interfaith co-operation to see how that work could help to bring peace to a world in turmoil and to ensure that the desperate needs of the poor were addressed. In Chicago itself, a Parliament of the World's Religions was held and the focus there also was on the vital relevance of interfaith co-operation in addressing the critical issues that face the world. In 'A Declaration Towards a Global Ethic', many members of the Parliament affirmed that, despite their differences, religions agree on core moral values.

The need now was to translate this agreement into policies that would effect real change. One way to do this, I thought, was to strengthen the co-operation of international interfaith organisations. I helped, therefore, to found the International Interfaith Centre, which was established in Oxford in December 1993. Now, some fourteen international interfaith organisations are linked in a network and there is a growing sense of partnership, although most member organisations, with small staff and inadequate finances, are hard-pressed to maintain their own work and have little spare energy for collaborative work. It was hoped that the centre would also facilitate research on the relevance of interfaith activity to the major challenges that face the world society. Some excellent conferences were held which focussed on the efforts of interfaith work in areas of conflict and peace-building, but this work has not been sustained.

The Council for a Parliament of the World Religions, following the 1993 Parliament, concentrated on how to engage the political, economic and scientific world with the religious world. A document entitled, 'A Call to the Guiding Institutions', to which I made a small contribution, was issued and became the focus for the 1999 Parliament of World Religions which was held in Cape Town. Similar issues were also to the fore at the 2004 Parliament in Barcelona, although the emphasis was on the practical measures that each individual participant could make to the problems.

In recent years, especially through my participation in the Three Faiths Forum, I have come to recognise that a growing number of politicians, economists and other leaders of society are now more aware of the influence – for good or ill – of religion on society. Some now also see that there is a spiritual and moral dimension to the urgent issues that the world faces. Interfaith organisations have helped to galvanise the world community to see the deeper causes of violence and terrorism, to be aware of the suffering caused by the widening gap between rich and poor, to recognise the urgency of cancelling the debt of poorer nations, to provide resources for the victims of Aids and other diseases, and to take measures to protect the environment. These efforts, however, have been seriously set back by the unwillingness of the present American government to take part in or to honour international agreements. Even more disastrous has been the war against Iraq – not only because of the immense loss of life and human suffering, but because it has undermined the authority of the United Nations and of international law.

It would be easy, as many people have, to despair. But a characteristic of faith in God is to hope that God's kingdom of righteousness and peace can be established. I go on hoping that a world society can be built on the moral and spiritual values which are to be found in all the great religious traditions. In dialogue, which is both multi-faith and multi-disciplinary, these values need to be translated into policies which will effect real change for the common good. This book is a plea for this. Many people across the world are engaged in this endeavour, but the work is fragmented and often not widely enough known. I still hope that a centre can be established which will be a focus for this work and which will encourage the efforts and prayers of so many people who believe that a world society can be created which treasures every human life – because each life is sacred and precious in the sight of God.

CHAPTER 4

✳

A reasonable estimate of economic organisation must allow for the fact that, unless industry is to be paralysed by recurrent revolts on the part of outraged human nature, it must satisfy criteria which are not purely economic.

R.H. TAWNEY

To attribute everything to the economic factor is to perpetuate the terrible lie of the Marxist. In addition to the economic is the political and, most important, the cultural. At the heart of the cultural is the moral and spiritual.

RICHARD JOHN NEUHAUS

Economic theory presupposes that each participant is a profit center bent on maximizing profits to the exclusion of all other considerations. But there must remain other values at work to sustain society – indeed human life. I contend that at the present moment market values have assumed an importance that is way beyond anything that is appropriate and sustainable. Markets are not designed to take care of the common interest.

GEORGE SOROS

The Roots of Economics
– And why it has gone so wrong

BY KAMRAN MOFID

P AUL ORMEROD, former Director of Economics at the Henley Centre for Forecasting, in his book *The Death of Economics* notes that:

Good economists know, from work carried out within their discipline, that the foundations of their subject are virtually non-existent... Conventional economics offer prescriptions for the problems of inflation and unemployment which are at best misleading and at worst dangerously wrong... Despite its powerful influence on public life, its achievements are as limited as those of pre-Newtonian physics ... It is to argue that conventional economics offers a very misleading view of how the world actually operates, and it needs to be replaced.

An equally accomplished economist, Mark Lutz, in his book *Economics for the Common Good* observes that:

Modern economics is the science of self-interest, of how to best accommodate individual behavior by means of markets and the commodification of human relations... In this economic world view, the traditional human faculty of reason gets short-changed and degraded to act as the servant of sensory desires. There is no room for logic of human values and rationally founded ethics. Human aspirations are watered down to skilful shopping behavior and channelled into a stale consumerism. One would think that there must be an alternative way to conceptualise the economy.

So what *is* economics? What are its roots? And why has it gone so wrong? In what follows I shall attempt to shed some light on these questions.

Economics has its origins in ancient Greece and its roots in ethics. Amartya Sen, in his significant study, *On Ethics and Economics*, demonstrates that, in its recent development, a serious distancing between economics and ethics has brought about one of the major deficiencies in contemporary economic theory. Sen argues that modern economics could become more productive by paying greater and more explicit attention to the ethical considerations that shape human behaviour and judgement. He observes a surprising contrast between the self-consciously non-ethical character of modern economics and its historical evolution as an offshoot of ethics.

The ethics-related tradition of economics goes back at least as far as Aristotle. It has been argued that Aristotle deserves recognition as the first economist, two thousand years before Adam Smith. Aristotle distinguished between two different aspects of economics: *oikonomikos* or household trading, which he approved of and thought essential to the working of any even modestly complex society, and *chrematisike*, which is trade for profit. He declared the latter activity wholly devoid of virtue and called those who engaged in such purely selfish practices 'parasites'. His attack on the unsavoury and unproductive practice of usury held force virtually until the fifteenth century, when John Calvin's writings started greatly to influence the study of economics.

The extension of Calvinism to all spheres of human activity was extremely important to a world emerging from an agrarian mediaeval economy into a commercial industrial cra. Calvin accepted the newborn capitalism and encouraged trade and production, while, most importantly, opposing the abuses of exploitation and self-indulgence. Industrialisation was stimulated by the concepts of thrift, industry, sobriety and responsibility that Calvin promoted as being essential to the achievement of the reign of God on earth.

However, in the eighteenth century, with the publication of Adam Smith's masterwork, *The Wealth of Nations*, there was a quantum leap in many aspects of economics. Now *chrematisike* became the driving force and primary virtue of modern society – a point to which I shall return later.

As Sen points out, at the very beginning of *The Nicomachean Ethics* Aristotle relates the subject of economics to human ends, referring to its concern with wealth. He sees politics as 'the master art' which must direct 'the rest of the sciences', including economics, and 'since, again, it legislates as to what we are to abstain from, the end of science must include those of the others, so that this end must be the good for man.'

Furthermore, according to Sen, the study of economics, though directly related to the pursuit of wealth, is at a deeper level linked to other studies which involve the assessment and enhancement of more basic goals. Quoting Aristotle, Sen notes that, 'the life of money-making is one undertaken under compulsion, and wealth is evidently not the good we are seeking; for it is merely useful and for the sake of something else.' Economics relates ultimately to the studies of ethics and politics, a point of view further developed in Aristotle's *Politics*.

The Penguin History of Economics defines economics as 'a science which studies human behaviour as a relationship between ends and scarce means with alternative uses'. I have collected some further definitions from the Web:

The branch of social science that deals with the production and distribution and consumption of goods and services and their management...   www.cogsci.princeton.edu

The science that deals with the production, distribution, and consumption of the worlds resources and the management of state income and expenditures in terms of money. www.sba.gov

Economics is the study of how men and society end up choosing, with or without the use of money, to employ scarce productive resources that could have alternative uses, to produce various commodities and distribute them for consumption, now or in the future, among various people and groups in society. It analyzes the costs and benefits of improving patterns of resource allocation. Economics is the study of the use of scarce resources to satisfy unlimited human wants.   hta.uvic.ca

The study of how individuals and societies choose to allocate scarce productive resources among competing alternative uses and to distribute the products from these uses among the members of the society.   www.worldbank.org

The study of choice and decision-making in a world with limited resources.   pittsford.monroe.edu

The science that deals with the production, distribution, and consumption of wealth, and with the various related problems of labour, finance, taxation, etc. [Webster's New World]

www.worldtrans.org

The study of how people use scarce resources to satisfy unlimited wants.   www.fiscalagents.com

The study of how scarce resources are allocated among competing uses.   www.lobsterconservation.com

The science of the allocation of limited resources for the satisfaction of human wants.   www.ptvincivilsociety.org

Study of how individuals, businesses and governments use their limited resources to satisfy unlimited wants.

www.turnerlearning.com

Economics is the study of ways in which people make a living; it considers the social organisation by means of which people satisfy their wants for scarce goods and services.

www.lcsc.edu

Study of how people choose to use scarce resources to satisfy their needs and wants; a study of choice.   www.radford.edu

The science that deals with the production, distribution, and consumption of commodities   www.fhsu.edu

The study of how persons and society choose resources which have alternative uses, to produce various commodities over time and distribute them for consumption now and in the future, among various people and groups in society.
                                            www.remaxescarpment.com

The social science that studies how individuals, firms, governments, and other organizations make choices, and how those choices determine the way the resources of society are used.
                                            wellspring.isinj.com

Economics provides the language, principles and a way of thinking to help people unravel why they have to make choices.
                                            www.cba.uc.edu

The study of supply and demand in markets and how they allocate scarce resources.   www.freebuck.com

The study of how resources are distributed for the production of goods and services within a social system.   www.mhhe.com

The study of how to distribute scarce resources among alternative ends.   highered.mcgraw-hill.com

The study of how limited resources, goods, and services are allocated among competing uses.   www.fs.fed.us

It is clear from the above that economics is perceived as a science concerned with scarcity, competition, production, consumption and the satisfying of unlimited desires. There is no reference to abundance, co-operation, sustainability, justice, compassion, humanity, morality or spirituality. No wonder it has brought us such a bitter harvest!

Economics defines ends and means primarily in material terms – essentially in monetary terms. Non-material, non-monetary values are considered subjective and therefore outside its scope. By stating that economic means are finite and scarce, economic theory accepts a natural element of competition for these resources. The textbooks tell us that man naturally competes for scarce and limited material resources. Happy is the man who is able to consume these resources, unhappy is the one who is not.

The assumptions underlying the so-called 'economic laws' were developed at a time when religion was being separated from science. The accepted world view was becoming secularised; the sacred was being replaced by a belief in matter. Economic theory was affected by the great scientific discoveries in physics, biology and psychology, and economic laws were presented with the same authority as laws of nature. Newton and Descartes described reality in terms of a more or less fixed number of 'building blocks', of 'things' subject to measurable laws such as gravity smartly put together so that they operated, as it were, mechanically. The world of matter was seen as a mere machine, to be used by man exercising his reason and free will. This world view has come to be known as 'scientific materialism'.

Over the last two centuries these principles have become firmly enshrined in our capitalist legal systems, domestically and internationally. For example, the international laws governing the main multilateral agency for international trade, the World Trade Organization, are based on Ricardo's concept of 'comparative advantage', the idea that nations, by specialising yet keeping their borders open, will benefit from unfettered competition. This idea arose in a seventeenth-century Europe which had invented the nation state to deal with the opportunities provided by colonial expansion.

With the emergence of the nation state, monetary systems and policies were developed based on the notion of a scarce money supply linked to gold and silver, the value of which was controlled by the nation. The artificial measurement of money scarcity, when the churches relaxed their restrictions on interest-bearing lending (denounced as 'usury' for many centuries), introduced an official element of competition among those in need of funding. Those with money could set the rules governing how scarce resources should be invested. Now enshrined in corporate and banking law (and underpinning what we know as 'capitalism'), these rules favour those with wealth over those who have nothing. The vast majority, the 'have nots', have ever since been locked into a vicious cycle of competition for scarce capital.

National political agendas continue to be determined by interest groups dominated by commerce and industry which are locked into old paradigms. The power of national authorities and national democratic institutions has been gradually eroded by the globalisation of industry, finance, technology and information.

The bodies that rule our global economy today, the G8 (the world's industrialised countries), the IMF and the World Bank (together known as the 'Washington consensus') prescribe for the world a neo-classical recipe of privatisation, decentralisation, deregulation and other market liberalisations, assuming that our common interests are best served by the invisible hand of the market.

Critics of this faith are silenced by powerful arguments that government interference in markets will lead to inefficient and wasteful government bureaucracies. They claim that history has shown that the libertarian or *laissez-faire* approach allows markets to increase wealth, promote innovation and optimise production – at the same time as regulating itself flawlessly. The fact that human beings persist in behaving 'irrationally and uneconomically', in terms of the market model, does not, they claim, invalidate that model: we simply have not yet learned to appreciate the benefits of competition.

Yet we can clearly see all around us that our economies are inherently flawed. The gap between rich and poor keeps growing in all societies, and also among the countries of the world. Environmental degradation seems irreversible. The drug trade and new forms of slavery prosper.

Corruption and corporate fraud are widespread; stock markets are turning into global casinos. War is increasingly 'economic', motivated by either the lack of or the protection of wealth. If the global economy does prosper, it is at the expense of the air, the earth, the water, our health and our rights to employment.

A further cause of disquiet is the mathematisation of human behaviour and the desire for predictive models. This is an important point in my argument as the over-reliance upon mathematical formulae is at the root of why economists have become detached from ethics, spirituality and theology in their professional studies. I will try to shed some light on this issue.

The use of mathematics in economics books and articles is very complex, no doubt very impressive. Along with physicists, economists seem to be those who rely most on advanced mathematical models, but there would appear to be a paradox here. Mathematics being synonymous with rigor and precision, how is it that it plays such a role in a discipline where vagueness reigns? The answer probably lies in the roots of this vagueness. Because the economic and social world is so difficult to grasp schematically, to reduce to simple laws, the temptation is to take refuge in fictitious worlds, in models which have little to do with what can actually be observed but which lend themselves to endless mathematical refinement. The most important of life's criteria and its purpose are ignored because economists are unable to fit them into their calculations for measurement.

How did mathematics come to assume such a dominating position in modern economics, with such a disastrous consequences? The blame can fairly and squarely be put at the door of Paul Samuelson.

In 1947 Samuelson, an assistant professor of economics at the Massachusetts Institute of Technology, published *Foundations of Economic Analysis*, a book which is considered to be the seminal work in the integration of mathematics and economics. While some economists had employed mathematics to some degree prior to this, Samuelson laid the groundwork for the complete 'mathematisation' of economics.

A natural consequence of this was the marginalisation of areas of research that could not be modelled using formal mathematics. By the early 1970s there had appeared a genuine chauvinism that belittled work not deemed to be serious enough, as measured by its mathematical content. This trend attracted increasing numbers of physicists, mathematicians and engineers into economics, which in turn nudged the level of 'mathematicality' up even further. Mathematicians were attracted to economics because it was mathematical in nature, and the field became even more mathematical because of their participation.

As I have said, the adverse effect of this trend is the neglect of fundamental issues by mainstream economists because they are deemed to be incapable of mathematical formalisation. Thus, notions of justice or ethical behaviour, which are not quantifiable, have no role in the current economic framework. The notion that firms seek to maximise profits is a cornerstone of economic analysis (and a sound one, as most firms do behave this way), but it begs the question what firms *ought* to do, based on ethical and moral grounds. Most economists spend no time at all exploring this alternative dimension of economic behaviour simply because it is not mathematically tractable.

To summarise, trends both internal to the discipline (such as the increased reliance on formal mathematics) and external (such as changes in political discourse) have moved the profession away from any attempt to deal with the ethical and moral dimensions of economic issues and policies. This trend has robbed the profession of a rich line of research that we have only recently starting to skirt around in our own research agenda.

It seems clear to me that the time has come for economics to change direction and to find a path which does not deviate from true human values. The obviously contrived nature of neo-classical economics has begun to attract many calls for change. One of the most vocal has come from university students. This is music to my ears. It is something I would very much like to share with you.

In the spring of 2000 an interesting dichotomy between theory and reality in economics teaching appeared in France when economics students from some of the most prestigious universities, including the Sorbonne, published a petition on the internet urging fellow students to protest against the way economics was being taught. They were against the domination of rationalist theories, the marginalisation of critical and reflective thought and the use of increasingly complex mathematical models. Some argued that the drive to make economics more like physics was flawed, and that it should be wrenched back in line with its more social aspects.

They called the economics they were being taught 'autistic' – divorced from reality – and called for a post-autistic economics that would 'rescue economics from its autistic and socially irresponsible state'. *Autisme-economie*, the Post-Autistic Economics (PAE) movement, was born.

Their letter of petition for change received important recognition when the French government agreed to set up a special commission to investigate its complaints. Below is the text of the petition, originally circulated in France in 2000 and now adopted by many other students in counties around the world.

Open letter from economics students to professors and others responsible for the teaching of this discipline

We declare ourselves to be generally dissatisfied with the teaching that we receive.

This is so for the following reasons:

1. We wish to escape from imaginary worlds!

Most of us have chosen to study economics so as to acquire a deep understanding of the economic phenomena with which the citizens of today are confronted. But the teaching that is offered, that is to say for the most part neoclassical theory or approaches derived from it, does not generally answer this expectation. Indeed, even when the theory legitimately detaches itself from contingencies in the first instance, it rarely carries out the necessary return to the facts. The empirical side (historical facts, functioning of institutions, and study of the behaviours and strategies of the agents ...) is almost nonexistent. Furthermore, this gap in the teaching, this disregard for concrete realities, poses an enormous problem for those who would like to render themselves useful to economic and social actors.

2. We oppose the uncontrolled use of mathematics!

The instrumental use of mathematics appears necessary. But resort to mathematical formalization when it is not an instrument but rather an end in itself, leads to a true schizophrenia in relation to the real world. Formalization makes it easy to construct exercises and to manipulate models whose significance is limited to finding 'the good result (that is, the logical result following from the initial hypotheses) in order to be able to write 'a good paper'. This custom, under the pretence of being scientific, facilitates assessment and selection, but never responds to the question that we are posing regarding contemporary economic debates.

3. We are for a pluralism of approaches in economics!

Too often the lectures leave no place for reflection. Out of all the approaches to economic questions that exist, generally only one is presented to us. This approach is supposed to explain everything by means of a purely axiomatic process, as if this were THE Economic Truth. We do not accept this dogmatism. We want a pluralism of approaches, adapted to the complexity of the objects and to the uncertainty surrounding most of the big questions in economics (unemployment, inequalities, the place of financial markets, the advantages and disadvantages of free-trade, globalization, economic development, etc).

4. Call to teachers: wake up before it is too late!

We appreciate that our professors are themselves subject to some constraints. Nevertheless, we appeal to all those who understand our claims and who wish for change. If serious reform does not take place rapidly, the risk is great that economics students, whose numbers are already decreasing, will abandon the field en masse, not because they have lost interest, but because they have been cut off from the realities and debates of the contemporary world.

**We no longer want to have this
autistic science
imposed on us.**

**We do not ask for the impossible,
but only that good sense may prevail.
We hope, therefore, to be heard very soon.**

The French students' cries for change were heard by the media. *Le Monde*, in an article of 13th September 2000, asked whether the teaching of economics in universities should not be rethought, and other French newspapers and magazines, as well as TV and radio stations, soon joined in the argument. The number of signatures on the petition rose significantly. The perceived seriousness of the controversy increased when, at the end of June 2000, a group of economics professors published their own a petition, backing the students and offering further analysis and evidence of the need for reform.

As is their wont, the neo-classical establishment – those with most to lose – began to cry foul. They tried to dismiss the petition as a Trotskyite conspiracy, espoused by *Le Monde*. Most of the backlash, as might have been expected, came from the neo-classical establishment in the US. What followed was an attempt to discredit the PAE by implying that the students were anti-intellectuals opposed to the 'scientificity' of neo-classical economics. The accusations, however, did not stick. The dissenters were top students who had done the maths and found it did not add up! This bankrupt and outdated form of attack, discrediting the messenger because you do not like the message, backfired. After malicious attacks were made at a major conference at the Sorbonne, a large group of economists convened to celebrate the fiftieth anniversary of the mainstream *La Revue Economique* and spontaneously deferred to issues raised by the reformists.

Among many in other countries who were inspired by the French students' rallying call were groups of PhD candidates and other students of economics at Cambridge and Oxford universities, who issued their own manifestos which recommended 'Opening Up Economics'. Similar groups have arisen elsewhere in Europe, the Americas and Australia.

Clearly we have to revisit the old assumptions. Are the laws of economics really uncontrollable? Spiritual teachers tell us that we make up reality; likewise it must be we who make up the economy. For better or for worse, businesses and economies don't function separately from our decisions: without us they wouldn't exist. If we want a better economic system we have to look deeply at who we are and how we live.

As an economist with a wide range of experience, I do appreciate the significance of politics, trade, banking, insurance and commerce – and of globalisation. I understand the importance of wealth-creation – but wealth must be created for a noble reason. I want to have a dialogue with the business and economic community. I want to listen to them and be listened to. Today's business leaders are in a unique position to influence what happens in society for years to come. With this power comes monumental responsibility. They can choose to ignore this responsibility, and thereby exacerbate problems such as economic inequality, environmental degradation and social injustice, but this will compromise their ability to do business in the long run. The world of good business needs a peaceful and just world in which to operate and prosper.

In order to arrive at this peaceful and prosperous destination we need to change the basis of neo-classical economics to take account of the common good. Many of the issues which people grapple with, or which their governments advocate, have economics at their core. The creation of a stable society in today's globalised world should not be ignored in favour of purely economic considerations of cutting costs and maximising profits. There are other fundamental values which must not be put aside.

John Maynard Keynes looked forward to a time when people in advanced economies would step back from traditional economic imperatives and feel free to concentrate on how to live wisely, agreeably and well. The purpose of the economy, according to Keynes, is to control the material basis of a civilised society, enabling its citizens to explore the higher dimensions of human existence, to discover their own full potential. In our world of prosperity for the few, we seem to have got that backwards. Lives are restricted by harsh working conditions and the common assets of a community are degraded in the pursuit of endless economic growth.

Economics must once again find its heart and soul. It must reconnect with its original source and once again become rooted in ethics and morality. The huge controversy which surrounds modern commercial activity arises because it does not adequately address the needs of the global collective, and so marginalises or excludes the powerless. Surely, in the interests of all, this has to change? There needs to be an explicit acknowledgment of universal values such as fairness, altruism, empathy and solidarity if economics is to work for the common good. Economics as practised today cannot by any stretch of the imagination claim to be for the common good. A revolution in values is needed. Economics and the business community must at the same time embrace both material and spiritual values.

Given the state of our world today, with its extremes of progress and poverty, it seems that modern economics, so elaborate and difficult to comprehend, so saturated with mathematical jargon and abstruse models and theories, has failed to deliver the happiness it promised because it has failed to satisfy people's real, spiritual needs. We have to reverse this. Let us not continue to construct a global society that is materially rich but spiritually poor. Let us work towards a globalisation for the common good by uniting spirituality and theology with economics.

Spiritual Views Rediscovered

AS WE ALL KNOW, spiritual traditions describe reality in terms rather different from those of traditional economic theory. The latter is concerned primarily with a mere fragment of human behaviour, our 'economic' actions, those which can be quantified in terms of money. The spiritual approach is to view reality holistically, to look at all the human actions – and even thoughts – that make up our being and society. Sander Tideman, a founder and executive chairman of Spirit in Business, a network promoting ethics and spirituality in the business world, has written extensively on this issue, and my own reflections below rely on his insights.

In economics textbooks human beings are seen as isolated consumers and producers interacting in markets driven by the pursuit of monetary gain. In spiritual traditions people are viewed as part of a larger whole with which they can communicate by opening their hearts and minds.

The new understanding of reality is systemic, which means that it is based not only on the analysis of material structures but also on the analysis of patterns of relationships among these structures and of the specific processes underlying their formation. This is evident not only in modern physics but also in biology, psychology and the social sciences. The understanding of modern biology is that the process of life essentially is the spontaneous and

self-organising emergence of new order, which is the basis
of life's inherent abundance and creativity. Life processes
are associated with the cognitive dimension of life, and
the emergence of new order includes the emergence of
language and consciousness.

Most economic strategies are based on the possession of
material things such as land, labour and capital. What
counts is how much property we own, how much money
we have and how many hours we work. The ideal for many
people is to own enough land and capital so that we don't
have to sell our time. This strategy, which will be recognised by many of us in developed countries, is based on the
assumption that land, labour and capital are all there is,
that the real world is a closed-end system. Spiritual traditions and modern sciences claim the opposite. They recognise the unlimited potential of every sentient being, the
potential to be whole and enlightened. Our minds create
and pervade everything, hence physical reality is accessible
to the spiritual.

Let us first examine this 'being' side of our existence.
What kind of beings are we? Happy or unhappy? Altruistic or selfish? Compassionate or competitive? Modest or
greedy? Driven to seek short-term pleasure or to seek
meaning, a higher purpose, a longer-term state of happiness? These are important questions on which economic
theory and spiritual traditions hold different views.

Economists have accepted the principles of selfish individualism: the more the individual consumes, the better-
off he will be. He consumes out of perpetual needs which,
if unmet, will make him innately unhappy. Economic
growth is achieved when individuals consume more and
more, demand boosting output. There is no room for altruism, where an individual may incur costs for no conceiv-
able benefit to himself. This approach sees co-operation as
a mere reciprocal arrangement among individuals. Individual sacrifices on behalf of the community are seen as an
insurance policy: they will ensure that the individual will

have a right to be helped by the community in the future.

We can all understand the need for a value such as compassion because of our mutual interdependence in an increasingly diminished and interconnected world, but spiritual traditions point to another, more profound and personal dimension to compassion. They advise us to make altruism the core of our practice, not only because it is the most effective insurance policy for our future, but specifically because the *real* benefit of compassion is that it will bring about a transformation in the mind of the practitioner. It will make us happy.

All religions promote love, compassion, altruism and service. A very good example is Sikhism, as Bhai Sahib Mohinder Singh will show in his Epilogue.

But how can we practise altruism if our real nature is selfish? Compassion can only work if our nature is receptive to an altruistic attitude, if somehow compassion is in harmony with our essence so that we actually *enjoy* being compassionate. If we are inherently selfish, surely any attempt to develop a compassionate attitude would be self-defeating?

Most religions state that mankind's nature is basically good — that our kind is kind. Buddhism explains that there is no independently existing self that is either good or bad. Our selfish motives are based on the illusion of an independent self which separates us from others. We may have selfish traits, they may even dominate us, but they can be removed with practice. And since we are connected to the world, since there is no disconnected self, the practice of compassion is most effective.

Modern scientific disciplines such as biology, psychology and medical science have started to study the effects of empathy on the human mind and body, on our health and relationships. Not surprisingly, they are discovering that compassion is of tremendous help to our sense of well-being. A compassionate frame of mind has a positive effect on our mental and physical health, as well as on our social life, while the lack of empathy has been found to cause or aggravate serious social, psychological and even physical disorders. Recent research on stress shows that people who seek only short-term pleasure are more prone to stress than those who seek a higher purpose, who seek meaning rather than pleasure.

Meaning generally is derived from actions such as serving others, going beyond immediate selfish needs. The fact that disregarding one's own short-term needs results in longer-term happiness turns the neo-classical economics notion of selfish individualism upside down.

The economist Stanislav Menchikov, as Tideman in *Compassion or Competition* has noted, remarks that:

The standard, neoclassical model is actually in conflict with human nature. It does not reflect prevailing patterns of human behavior ... If you look around carefully, you will see that most people are not really maximisers, but instead what you might call 'satisfiers': they want to satisfy their needs, and that means being in equilibrium with oneself, with other people, with society and with nature. This is reflected in families, where people spend most of their time, and where relations are mostly based on altruism and compassion. So most of our lifetime we are actually altruists and compassionate.

What does all this mean for our economy? Economic thinking is primarily focused on creating systems of arranging matter for optimal intake of consumption. It assumes that the main human impulses are competition and consumption, and it has side-stepped spiritual and moral issues because those would involve qualitative judgments on values and other intangibles that go beyond its initial premises. But, by assuming that the more we consume the happier we are, economists have overlooked the intricate workings of the human mind.

At the root of this belief in the market lies a very fundamental misconception. We have not really understood what makes us happy. Blind faith in economics has led us to believe that the market will bring us all the things we want. We cling to the notion that contentment is obtained by the senses, by sensual experiences derived from the consumption of material goods. This feeds an appetite of sensual desire. At the same time we are led to view others as our competitors, scrabbling for the same, limited resources as we are. So we experience fear – the fear of losing out, the fear that our desires will not be satisfied.

We can observe that the whole machine of expanding capitalism is fuelled by two very strong emotions: desire and fear. They are so strong that they appear to be permanent features of our condition. Yet many religious traditions have taught us that, since these emotions are based on ignorance, a misconception of reality, they can be removed by the true understanding of reality. According to religion, happiness is an inner or divine experience available to anyone, rich or poor. Fundamentally, there is nothing that we lack. By developing the mind, our inner qualities, we can experience perfect wholeness and contentment. If we share with others, we will find that we are not surrounded by competitors: others depend on us as we depend on them.

We need to recreate economic theory based on an understanding of what a human being really is and what makes him happy. As long as economics is based on a partial or wrong image of man and his reality, it will not produce the results we need.

In a sense, the redesigning of economic theory has already started. In order to explain the persistent tension between economic theory and practice, and recognising that conventional economics does not help us in our pursuit of happiness, old assumptions are being challenged. As a result, certain intangibles – such as values based on our more noble human impulses – are gradually entering the scope of leading thinkers, including historians, social scientists, businessmen and bankers – and even economists.

Nobel Prize-winning economist Douglass North says:

The theory employed, based on the assumption of scarcity and hence competition, is not up to the task. To put it simply, what has been missing [in economic theory] is an understanding of the nature of human coordination and cooperation

The 1998 Nobel Prize in Economics was awarded to Amartya Sen, who defines economic development in terms of the free supply of basic necessities such as education and health care. He contends that as long as the contemporary world denies elementary freedoms to the majority of its populations, planning for economic development is useless. He has thus restored an ethical dimension to the discussion of development. Sen writes, in *Development as Freedom*:

Along with the working of markets, a variety of social institutions contribute to the process of development precisely through their effects on enhancing and sustaining individual freedoms. The formation of values and social ethics are also part of the process of development that needs attention.

The 2003 Nobel Prize in Economics was awarded to Daniel Kahneman and the late Amos Tverski, both leading experts in behavioural finance. The latter challenged the Efficient Market Hypothesis, the dominant paradigm based on a mechanistic world view. As an extension, the nascent field of *neuroeconomics* seeks to ground economic decision-making in the biological substrate of the brain. Recent findings have provided direct empirical and quantitative support for economic models that acknowledge the influence of emotional factors on decision-making behaviour.

This was already clear to the economic historian David Landes when he noted that, 'If we learn anything from the history of economic development, it is that culture makes all the difference.' Just because markets give signals does not mean that people respond timely or well. Some people do so better than others; it depends on their culture. And culture is nothing but the aggregation of values.

CHAPTER 5

Bringing Economics and
Theology Together Again

BY MARCUS BRAYBROOKE

THE BASIC AGREEMENT of all religions about core
moral values is increasingly being recognised by religious leaders. It is urgent that these values are now
translated into practical policies that will reduce the economic inequalities in our world, bring relief to the very
poor, protect the environment and reduce the dangers of
violence and terrorism. Such policies can only result from
detailed co-operation between religious thinkers and economists, politicians, business leaders and members of other
relevant disciplines. Interfaith dialogue should also be
interdisciplinary dialogue.

Yet the thought of religion interfering with economic
and political life will be greeted with alarm and protest
by those who are afraid of the influence of extremists in the
world of Islam or of conservative evangelicals in the USA.

One of the criticisms levelled at Islam by many Western
writers is its failure to draw a separation between Church
and State. This separation, however, has contributed to the
privitisation of religion and the virtual absence of moral
considerations in political, economic and business life. The
divorce of ethics from economics and politics is dangerous
and some economists and business leaders are now recognising this. *Business Week*'s chief economist has said that 'A
New Economy needs a new morality ... there's a moral
vacuum at the heart of the New Economy that needs to be
filled.'[1] The guru of the World Economic Forum, George

Soros, has said the same, arguing that a purely transactional approach to economic activity governed by the
principle of self-interest, which he labels 'market fundamentalism', is in danger of undermining social values and
loosening moral constraints.[2]

This morality, I believe, should not be imposed. It needs
to be consensual and it needs to draw upon the moral
teaching of all the world religions and indeed should also
appeal to those who have no belief in God. Several valuable attempts to articulate what is often called 'a global
ethic' have already been made, but inevitably they are
expressed in general principles. If they are to have practical influence they need to be applied to economic policy.
Such application requires the combined efforts of theologians and economists.

Islam

ALTHOUGH IT IS TRUE that Islam does not distinguish
between the secular and the sacred, its position is more
nuanced than Western critics allow. Islam affirms that the
whole of life is under God's control and that all human
behaviour should be in obedience to God's will. A committed Christian might well say the same, but, in the West,
secular society has made a distinction between the sacred
and the profane. Sociologists have spoken of the 'privatis-
ing' of religion in the West, by which they mean that religious adherence has become a leisure-time activity – some
people go to church on a Sunday, other people go sailing
or shopping. Religion is seen as a personal choice and should
not interfere with politics or business. Indeed, a number of
Christians seem to 'compartmentalise' their lives. Their
religion is for their family life and weekends in leafy sub-
urbs, but is irrelevant to the boardroom or stock market.

Muslims traditionally do not make a distinction between
the sacred and the secular. It is the whole community which

should submit to God. This concern for a society that is obedient to God goes back to the Prophet Muhammad himself. At first he met with hostility and ridicule in Mecca, but in 622 CE he was invited to become leader of the neighbouring town of Madina. There he tried to create a community obedient to God and from Madina, in due course, he attacked and captured Mecca, which was to be ruled in accordance with the teaching that had been revealed to him. Muhammad, like Calvin later in Geneva, tried to shape a society that lived in obedience to God's word. The logic of this position is clear. If God is God, then all life should be lived in obedience to God's laws.

The early caliphs inherited Muhammad's role as 'commander of the faithful', but they were not 'messengers of God', as the prophet had been. The early caliphs combined spiritual and temporal leadership – as Christians would understand these terms. Gradually the political rulers of Islam lost their religious aura and the rulers came to be replaced, as the conscience-keepers of the community, by the *ulama* or learned men, who had studied the holy law in depth. In time only the first four caliphs came to be regarded as truly orthodox. The Umayyad dynasty (661-750) was seen as a reversion to secular kingship. The Abbasid caliphs, who ruled in Baghdad from 750 to 1258, had rather more prestige and some called themselves *Khalifat Allah* or God's deputy, or even 'the shadow of God upon earth' – phrases that would have shocked Muhammad. With the loss of effective power by the Abbasids in the tenth century, 'all genuine political authority in the mainstream Muslim tradition', writes Edward Mortimer, 'was secular', although developments in the Shi'ite tradition were rather different.[3] In the Sunni world 'virtue and justice', Mortimer adds, 'were no longer regarded as indispensable qualifications of a ruler.'[4] By the eleventh century most of the *ulama* were teaching that obedience was an absolute duty, even to an unjust ruler, since an unjust ruler was better than none at all.

Radical Muslims today reject these developments and insist that there should be no divorce between State and religion. They are therefore very critical of the life-style and secular policies of some Muslim rulers, often thought to be in the pay of the West. They have, with success in some countries, campaigned to replace legal codes, which they inherited from Western imperialist rulers, by the introduction of Shari'a – often in its harshest and most conservative form. (Too often Westerners are unaware that there are four different classic schools of Shari'a law.) As in the early days of Islam, many Muslims want to live in an Islamic state. Moreover, although Muslims, when they are in a minority, are taught to obey the laws of the country where they live, some groups, like the Muslim Parliament in Britain, hope that their country of residence will in due course become Muslim.

The Secular and the Sacred in Christianity

IN SOME WAYS, states where Islamic Shari'a law is rigidly enforced are reminiscent of mediaeval Christian society. 'The order of society' (in mediaeval Christendom), writes David Edwards, 'was at bottom upheld by religion... It was God who decreed the acceptance of the rights and duties of each grade in society. Indeed a sacred order or a "hier-archy" was thought to exist in the whole of God's creation.'⁵ Islamic societies were certainly not so hierarchical as feudal Europe but, just as the laws of Christendom were shaped by the Christian faith, so Shari'a law is based on the teach-ings of the Qur'an. In Christendom there were, of course, disputes about whether the sovereign or the Church should control society and at the Reformation there were radically different understandings of how to interpret the Christian faith. These differences were a cause of the prolonged religious wars of the sixteenth and seventeenth centuries.

From the seventeenth century, in reaction to these wars of religion, some politicians began to ignore moral constraints and to base their policies on 'reasons of state', which allowed a nation to deviate from the ethical norms required of the individual. Machiavelli (1469-1527) in his *Il Principe* (1513) had already argued for the 'self-preservation of the state with all means and at any price', which was equivalent to the 'suppression of any morality with a transcendent basis from the field of politics'.[6] But it was under Cardinal Richlieu (1585-1642) that, for the first time, in Hans Küng's words, 'reasons of state guided solely by political interests took the place of confessional interests and ethical considerations.'[7] Henry Kissinger, who greatly admired Richlieu's 'novel and cold-blooded doctrine', recognised that it 'was deeply offensive to the universalist tradition founded on the primacy of moral law … In an age still dominated by religious zeal and ideological fanaticism, a dispassionate foreign policy free of moral imperatives stood out like a snow-covered Alp in the desert.'[8]

Reaction to the wars of religion was also one of the factors which led to the separation of Church and State. For example, the United States of America, to which many of the first settlers had come to escape persecution, was, in 1791, the first Western nation to separate Church and State. Even today the teaching of religion in public schools is prohibited, although religious observance in the USA is far higher than in Europe. By contrast, in England there is still an established church – the Church of England. In the nineteenth century, the bishops in the House of Lords used their votes to delay the emancipation of Catholics and 'Dissenters', and of the Jewish people. Today they will often be a voice for the various faith communities but their position is certainly anomalous – but perhaps no more archaic than the House of Lords itself. In some Western European societies, such as The Netherlands, political life is partly moulded by Church allegiance. By contrast, in Communist countries the Church was stripped of political influence and in some, such as Albania, the practice of religion was illegal.

The situation differs from country to country. In some countries the Church still has considerable influence, but even where this is so it is disputed. It is therefore difficult to generalise about 'secularisation' – a word which itself is used in various senses. The term usually signifies the process by which religion loses social significance, but the emphasis may be on the relationship of Church and State or on the social influence of religion, or used to speak about individual belief and practice.[9]

The Enlightenment, with its assertion of the autonomy of human reason, is also a factor in the process of secularisation. Many of the leaders of the Enlightenment, such as Voltaire, Hume, Gibbon and Lessing, challenged Christianity. 'Dare to be adult and let go of the church's apron strings; trust your own reason and measure revelation against it; be prepared to use your own reason critically in any context,' as Alistair Mason summarises the Enlightenment's challenge to Christianity.[10] In Kant's words, the Enlightenment was 'the emergence of human beings from a tutelage to which they had voluntarily acceded.'[11]

Hans Küng suggests that the Enlightenment led to the unprecedented progress of the sciences, a completely new social order and a revaluation of the individual.[12] Today the Enlightenment approach is subject to strong criticism, especially from post-modernists, but it helped, for good or ill, to divorce political and economic thinking from a basis in a religious view of life.

But are the only alternatives religious zeal and ideological fanaticism on the one hand, and the absence of moral considerations and political cynicism on the other. Is there a third way? Indeed, Erasmus in the sixteenth century called for an ethically responsible, realistic peace policy, far removed from the mediaeval fanaticism of the Counter-Reformation or the cynicism of modern real politics.[13]

The key question for us, therefore, is whether politics

and economics are autonomous, or whether they should have a basis in a religious or moral view of the world. Is politics just the pursuit of power and national self-interest? Is economics just the attempt to maximise wealth?

This has been a continuing matter of debate. The view that they are not autonomous was clearly put by the nineteenth-century Anglican theologian F.D. Maurice, who said his job as a theologian was 'to dig, to show that the economy and politics have a ground beneath themselves, that society is not to be made anew by arrangements of ours, but is to be regenerated by finding the law and ground of its order and harmony and the only secret of its existence in God.'[14] This has been the view of many church people, perhaps most notably Archbishop William Temple, as Kamran Mofid indicates, and is also expressed in Vatican documents. Such an approach is evident also in Judaism and Islam and among Socially Engaged Buddhists and a growing number of Hindus.

A notable attempt to bring moral values to bear on international politics was President Wilson's peace programme at the end of the First World War, with its famous Fourteen Points. Wilson was, however, defeated by the self-interested cynicism of Clémenceau and Lloyd George, which almost inevitably sowed the seeds of further conflict. Political realism became dominant in the mid-twentieth century and found its classical expression in Hans J. Morgenthau's *Politics Among the Nations*, which was published in 1948. In contrast to what was labelled 'historical optimism', Morgenthau's realist theory rejects the view that 'a rational and moral political order, derived from universally valid principles, can be achieved here and now.'[15] The starting point is that human nature is driven by different contradictory forces and 'this being inherently a world of opposing interests and of conflict among them, moral principles can never be fully realised.'[16]

A similar attitude has developed in economic thinking. The 'realist' market theory, developed especially by Milton

Friedman, stresses competition. The market should be autonomous and left to its own self-regulating forces, without State intervention or moral constraints. Essentially, individuals should be allowed to pursue their economic interests freely, whether they choose to do so in a selfish or generous way. In 1970 Friedman chose, as a title for an article in the *New York Times Magazine*, 'The Social Responsibility of Business Is to Increase Its Profits'.[17]

F.A. Hayek, who was well aware of the complexity of economic development, also rejected any external moral standard by which economic activity should be judged. Brian Griffiths, summarising Hayek's view with which he does not agree, says that for Hayek

Ethics are not 'immutable and eternal', determined outside of the system, but the result of a process of adaptation to changing circumstances, namely cultural selection. It is precisely because there is no external moral standard that globalisation is considered an autonomous and amoral process, without the need for any system of governance.[18]

Hayek sees the growth of capitalism, including its moral systems and institutions, as spontaneous and not related to any external system of morals. Brian Griffiths suggests that Hayek's approach suffers from three weaknesses:

There would be no external standards of what is right and wrong, just and unjust, moral and immoral, by which its results could be judged; there would be no guarantee that, even in the absence of outside intervention, globalization would be a benign process; and there would be no assurance that in a free society, left to itself, we could count on an evolution of moral beliefs to generate values which would continue to underpin the market order.[19]

As we have suggested above,[20] leading figures in the business and economic world are warning of the danger of a moral vacuum. Religious thinkers, I believe, need to be more vocal in their support of those who affirm the need for political and economic life to be based on moral principles. They should encourage their followers to apply their moral convictions to the business and political world.

The question then becomes, who provides the values? In the past, most societies have been shaped by a dominant religion – or, in the twentieth century, by an ideology. Where people of more than one religion lived together, there was often a struggle for dominance. The subordinate group – such as the *dhimmi* in the Muslim world or Jews in those countries in mediaeval Europe where they were allowed to live – were tolerated under certain conditions. Indeed in Europe, where one Christian denomination was dominant, other Christians often suffered from discrimination and sometimes persecution.

Increasingly societies in the West are becoming multiracial and multi-faith. Some in Asia have been so for a long time. If one faith tradition seeks to dominate a multi-faith society, it is a recipe for social tension. Those who are the victims of discrimination will feel alienated and may seek to subvert existing political structures. In some cases they will do this by peaceful protest, sometimes by violent action.

A Global Ethic

IS THERE a third way? Without some shared values, a society falls apart. If there is no concept of truth, business agreements become impossible – and indeed the presence of lawyers at every negotiation today are a sign that trustworthiness has been too much undermined. But even a legal system is an expression of underlying values. A society – and this is also true of our international society – needs values, but in a multi-faith society and world, if they are imposed by one faith community, even if it is the majority faith community, this will be resented and these values are likely to prove divisive. This is why it is urgent that faith communities articulate the values that they have in common in what is often now called 'a global ethic'.

Many spiritual leaders recognise the need for such a global ethic. Muslims, Buddhists, Jews, Hindus, Jains and others, as well as Christians, have said 'Yes' to a global ethic.[21] Let Pope John Paul II serve as an example. In 2001, he said:

As humanity embarks upon the process of globalisation, it can no longer do without a common code of ethics ... This does not mean a single dominant socio-economic system or culture which would impose its values and its criteria on ethical reasoning. It is within man as such, within universal humanity sprung from the Creator's hand, that the norms of social life are to be sought. Such a search is indispensable if globalisation is not to be just another name for the absolute relativisation of values and the homogenization of life-styles and cultures. In all the variety of cultural forms, universal human values exist and they must be brought out and emphasised as the guiding force of all development and progress.[22]

The best known effort to produce a global ethic is the declaration that was signed by most members of the 1993 Assembly of the Parliament of the World's Religions. At a time of intense conflict in former Yugoslavia, and of communal trouble in India, the Parliament sought to show that religions need not be a cause of division but could unite on basic ethical teachings. Much of the immediate preparatory work for this had been done by Professor Hans Küng, but interfaith organisations for some years had been working to identify the basic agreement of different religions on moral values.[23]

It is important to be clear that the global ethic is not intended to be a substitute for the specific moral teaching of particular religions. Hans Küng himself says:

The global ethic is no substitute for the Torah, the Gospels, the Qur'an, the Bhagavad Gita, the Discourses of the Buddha or the Teachings of Confucius and other scriptures. [It is concerned

simply with a] minimal basic consensus relating to binding values, irrevocable standards and moral attitudes which can be
affirmed by all religions despite their dogmatic differences and
can also be supported by non-believers.[24]

Certainly the ethical element in a religion has to be
understood in the context of the whole. 'The source of
vision and motivation for people of religious belief is their
experience of the supreme reality, the transcendent, or the
divine.'[25] Moral concern cannot be separated from inner
transformation, but, as twentieth-century religious leaders
of several traditions have insisted, such inner transformation also embraces a concern for the well-being of the
whole society. Mahatma Gandhi said, 'The only way to find
God is to see him in his creation and to be one with it. This
can only be done by service of all, *sarvodaya*.'[26] The Dalai
Lama has also spoken of 'compassion in action' and Rabbi
Soetendorp of the Netherlands has spoken of 'prayers with
legs'.[27]

Although for most believers their ethical conduct is part
of their whole faith commitment, it is I believe possible to
recognise fundamental agreements, which the global ethic
attempts to express. Indeed, the Golden Rule is to be
found in almost all religious traditions. In the same way, as
I argued in the introduction to *Stepping Stones to a Global
Ethic*, the contemporary concern for human rights, even if
expressed in the thought forms of the Enlightenment, is
grounded in faith traditions.[28]

It may be that attempts so far to articulate universal
human rights and to identify a global ethic have been too
much expressed in Western thought forms. This does not
invalidate the efforts, but it indicates that wider participation is necessary to improve them. Both the books, *For All
Life*, which Leonard Swidler edited, and *Testing the Global
Ethic*, which Peggy Morgan and I edited, include comments
on the global ethic from members of several world religions.
The task, as Leonard Swidler makes clear, is not complete:

But when the *Universal Declaration of a Global Ethic* is finally drafted – after multiple consultation, revision and eventual acceptance by the full range of religious and ethical institutions – it will serve as a minimal ethical standard for humankind to live up to, much as the United Nation's 1948 *Universal Declaration of Human Rights*. Through the former, the moral force of the world's religions and ethical institutions can be brought to bear especially on those issues which are not susceptible to the legal and political force of the latter.[29]

Does the global ethic appeal only to those with a religious faith? Hans Küng made clear that the intention was that it should be 'convincing and practical for all women and men of good will, religious and non-religious'.[30] The underlying principle, therefore, was that

... every human being must be treated humanely ... This means that every human being without distinction of age, sex, race, skin colour, physical or mental ability, language, religion, political view, or national or social origin possesses an inalienable and untouchable dignity ... Humans ... must be ends, never mere means, never objects of commercialization and industrialization in economic, politics and media.[31]

For me, as a Christian, this emphasis on treating every human humanely resonates with words attributed to Jesus: 'I came that they might have life and have it in all its fullness.'[32] Augustine said, 'The glory of God is man fully alive,' and several Christian writers have claimed that Christianity is the true humanism. Likewise members of other faiths have shown that there is support for the global ethic in their tradition. Certainly the principle 'treat every human humanely', which is really the Golden Rule, can be found in most faith traditions, although the scriptural or theological support for this statement will be particular to each faith. It is also a principle that should appeal to many people who have no belief in a transcendent reality.

It is, of course, a very general principle and in the *Declaration Toward a Global Ethic* an attempt was made to give it more substance. Four 'Irrevocable Directives' were affirmed, based on this fundamental demand that every human being must be treated humanely.

They are:

1 Commitment to a culture of non-violence and respect for life.

2 Commitment to a culture of solidarity and a just economic order.

3 Commitment to a culture of tolerance and a life of truthfulness.

4 Commitment to a culture of equal rights and partnership between men and women.

'Commitment to a culture of solidarity and a just economic order' is, of course, still very general. People of faith may disagree sharply about how to implement this. Indeed, this can be seen in current debates on how to make globalisation good. For example, the Hindu reformer Swami Agnivesh puts the dilemma very clearly:

There are two radically different approaches to dealing with the issue of human greed. The first is to put in place checks and balances so that the predatory and exploitative instincts in human nature do not become socially subversive. This approach is centred in law...

The second approach, however, rejects this assumption and assumes that the persistence of greed and its power over individuals and societies stems from a materialistic world view. If lust for material acquisition can be tempered with love for one's fellow human beings and accountability to God, it becomes possible to deal with the problem of greed effectively.[33]

This is a question that needs to be discussed together by religious thinkers and economists – especially economists who are themselves people of faith.

There are many other and more practical issues that also need to be discussed by religious thinkers and economists.

Some religious leaders call for those in the affluent world to adopt a simpler lifestyle. But would reduction of consumption in the West, on a large scale, really transfer resources to those who live in poverty, or would it trigger a recession? What is the goal of development? The views of the World Bank and of faith communities are often very different?[34]

A great deal of study and discussion is taking place, but groups often work in isolation. A centre is needed to ensure that the fruits of these efforts are better co-ordinated and communicated to the faith communities so that they have a real impact on a dangerous and divided world. There is a feeling among some interfaith activists that the 2004 Parliament of World Religions in Barcelona, for all its achievements, missed the opportunity to be the catalyst for this necessary development.

The editors of *Interreligious Insight* ask readers to

Imagine a world in which religious and spiritual communities regularly and creatively engage with other powerful and influential institutions to build a better future for all. Imagine a world in which the deepest wisdom and values of the great spiritual traditions touch the critical questions of the age, and in which religious communities are in deep and thoughtful dialogue with experts on all those critical questions.[35]

We need to make this vision a reality. If those who believe that economics should serve the good of all people, and should be based on and reflect the moral values upheld by the great religions, are to have a practical impact then religious thinkers and economists need to work together on detailed policies which embody these moral values. It will then be possible, as with the Jubilee 2000 campaign, to focus on specific issues and win popular support. It is time for the global ethic and talk of Globalisation for the Common Good to move from the conference hall to the political agenda.

REFERENCES

1 Michael Mandel in *Business Week*, 25th February, 2002, p.115.
2 Quoted by John Dunning in *Making Globalization Good*, p.32, referring to G. Soros, *The Crisis of Global Capitalism*, Little, Brown & Co, London, 1998, p.75.
3 E. Mortimer, *Faith and Power in the Politics of Islam*, Faber & Faber, 1982, p.37.
4 *Ibid.*
5 David L. Edwards, *Religion and Change*, Hodder & Stoughton, 1969, p.57.
6 H. Munkler, *Machiavelli*, Frankfurt, 1982, pp.283 and 281, quoted by H. Küng, *A Global Ethic for Global Politics and Economics*, SCM Press, 1997, p.17.
7 H. Küng, *A Global Ethic for Global Politics and Economics*, p.16.
8 H. Kissinger, *Diplomacy*, New York, 1994, pp.62 and 63.
9 Hugh McLeod, 'Secularization' in *The Oxford Companion to Christian Thought*, ed. Adrian Hastings, Oxford University Press, 2000, pp.653-4.
10 Alistair Mason, 'Enlightenment', in *The Oxford Companion to Christian Thought*, pp.200-1.
11 I. Kant, *Werke VI*, 53-61:53, quoted by H. Küng, *The Religious Situation of Our Time*, SCM Press, 1995, p.684.
12 H. Küng, *The Religious Situation*, p.687
13 Quoted by H. Küng, *A Global Ethic for Global Politics and Economics*, p.20, with reference to his *Christianity*, C IV5.
14 Quoted by S.C. Carpenter, *Church and People, 1789-1889*, SPCK, 1959 edn, Part II, pp.317-18.
15 H.J. Morgenthau, *Politics Among Nations: The Struggle for Power and Peace*, New York, 1948, 1961 edn, p.4.
16 H.J. Morgenthau, *Politics Among Nations*, p.4.
17 *New York Times Magazine*, 9th September 1970, quoted by Küng, p.191.
18 Brian Griffiths, 'A Christian Perspective' in *Making Globalization Good*, ed. John Dunning, Oxford University Press, 2003, p.168.
19 Brian Griffiths, p.168.
20 See p.43.
21 See *Yes to a Global Ethic*, ed. Hans Küng, SCM Press, 1996.
22 Pope John Paul II in an Address to the Papal Academy of Social Sciences, 27th April 2001, Vatican website.
23 See *Stepping Stones to a Global Ethic*, ed. Marcus Braybrooke, SCM Press, 1992, and *For All Life*, ed. Leonard Swidler, White Cloud Press, Ashland, Oregon, 1999.
24 Hans Küng, *A Global Ethic for Global Politics and Economics*, p.109.
25 See *Millennium Challenges for Development and Faith Institutions*, Katherine Marshall & Richard Marsh, The World Bank, 2003.
26 Mahatma Gandi, *Harijan*.
27 Quoted by David Johnston in *Interreligious Insight*, Vol. 2, No. 4, October 2004, p.15.
28 Louis Henken said that 'all major religions proudly lay claim to fathering human rights.' Louis Henken, *The Rights of Man Today*, Westview Press, 1978, p.xii. Likewise, Section 4 of the report *Poverty and Development* says that 'the present articulation of human rights is a secular formation of the

spiritual notion of the dignity inherent to each person, and thus has its grounding in the basic principles of all religions.'

29 *For All Life*, ed. Leonard Swidler, p.18.
30 *A Global Ethic*, ed. Hans Küng and Karl-Josef Kuschel, SCM Press, 1993, p.21.
31 *ibid.*, p.23.
32 *John* 10.10.
33 Swami Agnivesh in *Subverting Greed*, ed. Paul Knitter & Chandra Muzaffar, Orbis, 2002, pp.50-1.
34 See *Millennium Challenges for Development and Faith Institutions*.
35 *Interreligious Insight*, Vol. 2, No. 4, October, 2004, p.7.

FURTHER READING

Barney, Gerald, *Threshold 2000*, CoNexus Press, 2000.
Braybrooke, Marcus (ed.), *Stepping Stones to a Global Ethic*, SCM Press, 1992.
Camilleri, Joseph A. & Chandra Muzaffar (eds). *Globalisation: The Perspectives and Experiences of the Reliogious Traditions of Asia Pacific*, International Movement for a Just World, Malaysia, 1998.
Day, Herman E. & John B. Cobb, *For the Common Good*, Beacon Press, Boston, 1989, revised edn 1994.
Dunning, John, *Making Globalization Good*, Oxford University Press, 2003.
Edwards, David L., *Religion and Change*, Hodder & Stoughton, 1969.
Heslam, Peter (ed), *Globalization and the Good*, SPCK, 2004.
Knitter, Paul & Chandra Muzaffar (eds). *Subverting Greed*, Orbis, 2002.
Küng, H., *A Global Ethic for Global Politics and Economics*, SCM Press, 1997.
Küng, H., *Global Responsibility*, SCM Press,1993.
Küng, H., *The Religious Situation of Our Time*, SCM Press, 1995, p.687.
Küng, Hans (ed.), *Yes to a Global Ethic*, SCM Press, 1996.
Küng, Hans & Karl-Josef Kuschel (ed.), *A Global Ethic*, SCM Press, 1993, p.21.
Marshall, Katherine & Richard Marsh. *Millennium Challenges for Development and Faith Institutions*, The World Bank, 2003.
Millennium Challenges for Development and Faith Institutions, The World Bank, 2003.
Morgenthau, H.J., *Politics Among Nations: The Struggle for Power and Peace*, New York, 1961.
Mortimer, E., *Faith and Power in the Politics of Islam*, Faber & Faber, 1982.
Soros, G., *The Crisis of Global Capitalism*, Little, Brown & Co, London, 1998.
Swidler, Leonard (ed.), *For All Life*, White Cloud Press, Ashland, Oregon 1999.

CHAPTER 6

Ideals into Practice
Reuniting economics and theology

BY KAMRAN MOFID

THIS CHAPTER introduces a difficult but inescapable question central to my thesis: what place is there for religion and religious values in the global economy, and what should the relationship between economics and theology be? This is a vital and timely question given the rise of fundamentalism across the world, which gave us 9/11 and the wars in Afghanistan and Iraq. Religions represent some of the oldest and most enduring global networks, rooted as they are in vigorous ethical, moral and spiritual principles which are strangers to the global neo-liberal market. One must ask whether they could not offer insights to those responsible for creating the global economy and point the way towards a consideration of the common good.

Like others promoting a dialogue between religion and economics (such as Lorna Gold in *The Sharing Economy*), I believe that there must be a place for religion in our quest to find solutions to the deepening crises of injustice and inequality in the globalised economy. The relationship between economics and theology is one that needs to be taken seriously as we search for alternative socio-economic models.

What has theology to do with the economy? From the standpoint of the average economics textbook of today (as D. Stephen Long observes in *Divine Economy*), the answer is

61

absolutely nothing. As I have pointed out in *Globalisation for the Common Good*, modern neo-liberal economics tolerates religion only when religion narrows its focus to questions of individual salvation; the wider social concerns which preoccupied Moses, Jesus, Mohammed and other prophets are not considered to be within its realm. For neo-liberal economists anything that interferes with their own god and religion, the marketplace, is blasphemous.

What has the economy to do with theology? Again as Long has observed, despite the economists' neglect of theology, a number of theologians are now studying the relationship between theology and economics. In doing so, they continue in an ancient tradition which believes that faith and economic matters are inextricably linked. This is a significant movement because it runs contra to the development of modern economics, which has become increasingly anti-humanistic.

Political economists first divorced economics from theology at the end of the eighteenth century, and economists of the nineteenth century went on to free it from political theory. It was in the twentieth century that the subject of economics became increasingly abstract, de-humanised and mathematical.

All of us who care about both faith and economics are indebted to those theologians who are getting to grips with economics because the gravest temptation we face is the rending asunder of theology and economics – if this process were to be completed an ancient tradition would disappear.

Peter Milward SJ eloquently observes that we are only just beginning to understand how intimately and profoundly the vitality of a society is bound up with its religion. The religious impulse unifies a society and culture. The great civilisations of the world do not produce the great religions as a kind of cultural by-product; in a very real sense, the great religions are the foundations on which the great civilisations rest. A society which has lost its religion and its spirituality becomes a society which has lost its culture, and sooner or later it will fail to exist, as have many civilisations in the past.

Vaclav Havel came to the same conclusion during his years in prison before he was President of Czechoslovakia:

I am persuaded that [the present global crisis] ... is directly related to the spiritual condition of modern civilisation. This condition is characterised by loss: the loss of metaphysical certainties, of an experience of the transcendental, of any super-personal moral authority, and of any kind of higher horizon. It is strange but ultimately quite logical: as soon as man began considering himself the source of the highest meaning in the world and the measure of everything, the world began to lose its human dimension and man began to lose control of it.

In *The Secularism of the West*, Father Neuhaus observes:

The great question is whether modernity and liberal democracy can be secured in ways compatible with vibrant religious faith. That question is answered by remembering how, in historical fact, these achievements were secured. While modernity and democracy sometimes met with ecclesiastical resistance, they were generally inspired by religious conviction. From Magna Carta in 1215 through the Cromwellian revolution to the Declaration of Independence and its appeal to 'Nature and Nature's God,' the champions of freedom have invoked transcendent truth in the vindication of their cause. Accurately told, it becomes evident that religion is not the enemy but the foundation of modernity and freedom.

Robert Wuthnow in *Religion and Economic Life* notes:

Whether there may be residues of ethical or value oriented reasoning in religious traditions capable of suggesting ways of restricting economic commitments is thus an additional cause for rethinking the relationship between religion and economic life.

In *God and Mammon in America*, Wuthnow explains:

Materialism … is a problem that connotes selfishness, an individualistic emphasis on self-interest that devalues the community and the need to care for others. Selfishness is a problem, in turn, because religious traditions champion love, compassion, reaching out to the community, caring for others. It is this, more than anything else about religion in contemporary society, that butts up against the pervasive materialism to which we are exposed.

As these inspiring quotations suggest, there should be a natural kinship between economics and theology and among economists and theologians. Lack of such a dialogue is clearly a great shortcoming on the part of all concerned and it has to be put right.

A Call for a Theological Economics

THE DIFFICULTIES created by the secularisation of Western society, particularly in academia, have been analysed by many. Theological reflection is particularly scarce within economics, and most of what there is is outside the professional mainstream. This is strange considering the roots of economics were in theology.

Understanding the interrelationship of economics and theology is not easy: it requires a deep understanding of both. While I do not pretend to have mastered the two disciplines, what I do know is that they need to be reunited so that they can work together for the common good.

On the first page of his *Principles of Economics*, Alfred Marshall wrote:

Man's character has been moulded by his every-day work, and the material resources which he thereby procures, more than by any other influence unless it be that of his religious ideals; and the two great forming agencies of the world's history have been the religious and the economic.

Keynes in his introduction to his *Essays in Persuasion* expressed his conviction that:

... the Western World ... [is] capable of reducing the economic problem, which now absorbs our moral and material energies, to a position of secondary importance ... [T]he day is not far off when the Economic Problem will take the back seat where it belongs, and ... the arena of the heart and head will be occupied, or re-occupied, by our real problems – the problems of life and of human relations, of creation and behaviour and religion.

Thus it seems that, according to great economic minds, religion and economics are formative agencies that shape human society and the conduct of human affairs. My own argument for a theological economics weaves together several strands of thought inspired by many others before me. Above I quoted Marshall and Keynes, but the idea of a theological economics is much older.

As Waterman, for example, has observed, by far the most influential theodicy in the Christian West is that of St Augustine of Hippo, whose voluminous and powerful writings set the theological agenda for more than a thousand years. Augustine began with the Pauline doctrine of original sin and the fall of man, and attributed all moral evil, and most if not all physical evil, to that. What, then, does God do about it? Augustine's answer was complex, but his account of political society is very useful for the purpose of this study. The State and its institutions are seen as a self-inflicted punishment for human sin. Augustine had no illusions about the human cost of maintaining internal peace and external security, but without justice the State is an unmitigated evil: *'Remota itaque justitia, quid sunt regna nisi magna latrocinia?'*

Because of human sin, true justice is never fully obtainable: *'vera autem justitia non est nisi in en re publica cuius conditor rectorque Christus est'*. Yet some degree of justice remains possible, so God allows the self-regarding acts of sinful human beings to bring the State into existence because its institutions – especially those of private property, marriage and slavery – are also a remedy for sin. By means of the State, the evil in human life may be constrained to that minimum that must result from freedom of the will in fallen humanity. Waterman suggests that there are parallels between this aspect of St Augustine's theodicy and the account we may read in Adam Smith's *Wealth of Nations*, a point to which I shall return later.

As Paul Oslington notes, St Augustine spoke of the city of God which is entwined with the city of this world. For us the most relevant aspect of his work is not the political relationship between the two cities, but his comments on the relationship between theology and his classical Greek and Roman philosophical heritage. Augustine's problem – how to relate the claims of theology to a system of thought which had become his own after many years of training – is in many ways similar to our problem of how to reconcile theology and economics. His solution, which commends itself to us, was that the classical heritage need not be discarded; it should be utilised, and in fact finds its full meaning in the light of Christian theology.

Many centuries later John Henry Newman, in part stimulated by the Tractarian controversies over the rival claims of the State and secular learning versus the claims of theology, came to a similar conclusion about the primacy of theology without having to reject secular learning. For Newman all knowledge is one, and the sciences, including theology, form a circle of knowledge. Theology and the other disciplines all suffer loss if any is removed from the circle, or if any tries to usurp the place that properly belongs to another. In *The Idea of a University* he views the new discipline of political economy as valuable in its proper place but showing dangerous tendencies towards usurping the domains of ethics and theology.

Oslington further remarks that, in our own century, Harry Blamires in 1963 exhorted us to seek a Christian mind which relativises the claims of secular science. John Stott in 1983 attempted to establish the content of such a mind in more detail. Leslie Newbig a few years later, in his writings about the nature of a missionary encounter between the Gospels and Western culture, questioned the confinement of the claims of Christian theology to a private world and the trivialisation of them as matters of opinion or personal taste.

Adam Smith is, as noted, the mentor of neo-classical economists: they love to be associated with him, claiming legitimacy for right-wing policies by stressing the importance of individual liberty. They have taken no time to understand Smith's spirituality and how his theology might have influenced his own true values. Are the values of the neo-classicists and those of Smith really the same? They cannot be, given that the neo-liberals ignore Smith's religious dimension.

It is worth repeating that economics, from the time of Plato through to Adam Smith and John Stuart Mill, was as deeply concerned with issues of social justice, ethics and morality as with economic analysis itself. However, economics students today are taught that Adam Smith was the 'father of modern economics' but not that he was also a moral philosopher. The theological aspects of Adam Smith's economics have been discussed by Viner, Minowitz and Waterman, amongst others. Within the limitations of my present study, I will attempt to provide a summary only, based mainly on Waterman.

He remarks that, were we to re-read Smith's 'great book', *The Wealth of Nations*, with proper attention, we could learn from his 'interesting mind' a lot more than 'its owner wished to teach us'. Because the book may be read – and conceivably was sometimes read – as a work of 'natural theology', rather as Newton's *Principia* was read by Cambridge undergraduates for most of the eighteenth century. In *The Wealth of Nations* Adam Smith observes that 'Commerce ... ought naturally to be, among nations, as among individuals, a bond of union and friendship.' But, because of 'the capricious ambition of kings and ministers' and 'the impertinent jealousy of merchants and manufacturers', it has become 'the most fertile source of discord and animosity'. Neither the 'violence and injustice of the rulers of mankind' nor 'the mean rapacity ... of merchants and manufacturers' can be 'corrected' (though the latter 'may very easily be prevented from disturbing' the tranquillity of others) because they are evils for which 'the nature of human affairs can scarce admit of a remedy'.

In this passage, especially in the phrase 'the nature of human affairs', Smith comes close to the traditional doctrine of original sin. In describing its putative consequences, his language is more highly coloured than usual. He assails the 'savage injustice' of European colonisation of the New World. 'All for ourselves and nothing for other people seems, in every age of the world, to have been the vile maxim of the masters of mankind.' Feudal proprietors were driven by 'the most childish, the meanest and the most sordid of all vanities'. The 'great lords' beheld the growing prosperity of the burgesses – their former serfs – with a 'malignant and contemptuous indignation'.

The protective legislation 'which the clamour of our merchants and manufacturers has extorted ... may be said to have been all written in blood'. Even relatively minor vices – profusion, prodigality and extravagance – draw strong moral condemnation. The 'prodigal' perverts capital 'from its proper destination'. 'Like him who perverts the revenues of some pious foundation to profane purposes, he pays the wages of idleness with those funds which the frugality of his forefathers had, as it were, consecrated to the maintenance of industry.' Such language makes sense only if we assume that 'the original principles in human nature' are seen to be good, that traces of a 'common humanity' remain, that humans have genuine free will, and that intentional deviation by individuals from what is natural is culpable.

Adam Smith shows great respect and affection for his church, praising 'the equality which the Presbyterian form of church government establishes among the clergy'. For equality among the clergy supplies incentives that reward 'learning', 'irreproachable regularity' of life, and 'diligent discharge' of duty. Consequently, 'There is scarce perhaps to be found anywhere in Europe a more learned, decent, independent, and respectable set of men, than the greater part of the Presbyterian clergy of Holland, Geneva, Switzerland, and Scotland.'

Smith concludes his remarkable Providentialist account of 'the natural course of things' (which by enlisting 'interest' can bring good out of evil in a manner impossible through 'the feeble efforts of human reason'), with his ringing tribute to his national church:

The most opulent church in Christendom is no better at maintaining the uniformity of faith, the fervour of devotion, the spirit of order, regularity and austere morals in the great body of the people, than the poorly endowed Church of Scotland. All the good effects, both civil and religious, of an established Church are produced by it as much as any other.

One may construe *The Wealth of Nations* as containing, and possibly even as being shaped by, a quasi-Augustinian account of the way in which God responds to human sin by using the consequences of sin both as a punishment and as a remedy. It is evident that Smith's theology is 'natural theology', a knowledge of God arrived at by the study of nature alone, without any reliance on 'revelation' as recorded in sacred scripture.

'Nature' is almost always viewed theologically in *The Wealth of Nations*. It has a purpose, and part of that purpose is human welfare. This implies either a transcendent Newtonian God of Nature or an immanent Leibnitzian God *in* Nature. Smith does not say which but, though his text is capable of either interpretation, it is easier to read it in the second of these ways. Even given the first interpretation, however, Smith's putative God/Nature is not merely 'the great machine' the Deists believed Nature to be. She continues to act in various ways, but always wisely and well, making creative use of human folly and wickedness in ways that bring good out of evil.

Such redemptive activity, we may assume, is necessary only because humans have been endowed by God/Nature with the freedom to choose and, though intended to choose well, have a universal, perhaps primordial, failing that impels them often to choose ill. Natural theology is ecumenical: its truths are available to all who will read the 'Book of Nature', whatever their religious tradition. Yet it would be a mistake to imagine that, in eighteenth-century Britain, natural theology would have been regarded as in any way opposed to or inconsistent with Christianity.

Smith's great exemplar was Newton, and the Newtonian character of *The Wealth of Nations* has been remarked from the first. Newton published his *Principia* in 1687 'with an Eye upon such Principles as might work with considering Men for the belief of a Deity'. Throughout the eighteenth century, Newton was read by Cambridge men preparing for Holy Orders in the Church of England as part of their theological training. By the time of Malthus they did so with the help of Colin Maclaurin's popularising textbook. According to Maclaurin, we learn from Newton that 'Our views of Nature ... represent to us ... that mighty power which prevails throughout, ... wisdom which we see ... displayed, ... the perfect goodness by which they are evidently directed'.

Waterman remarks that much has been made by some authors of the fact that there is no mention in *The Wealth of Nations* of 'Jesus', 'Christ', or 'the Son'. But neither is there any mention of that Person in the *Principia*, and it would never have occurred to any of Newton's readers for that reason to describe his work as an 'atheistic science'. The aim of natural theology is to show by means of a scrupulously positive ('objective', 'secular', 'ecumenical') inquiry that knowledge of God may be had without resort to revelation. It is clear from our knowledge of the theological training of the Christian clergy in eighteenth-century Scotland and England that natural theology formed an important prolegomenon to the more doubtful and controverted mysteries of revealed religion. Smith himself taught natural theology as Professor of Moral Philosophy at Glasgow but, before doing so, publicly assented to the Calvinist Confession of Faith before the Presbytery of Glasgow.

After this brief, but I hope useful, reflection on the theological aspects of Adam Smith's economics, I shall now attempt to provide a short summary of the various positions taken on the relationship between Christian theology and economics. People of other religious traditions have wrestled with issues similar to those concerning their Christian counterparts when confronting economics and theology. As examples concerns from the Muslim and Jewish traditions will be highlighted.

The literature on the relationship between Christianity and capitalism is, as noted by Gold, vast indeed. Much of it draws on the tradition of writers such as Max Weber, which underlines the ways in which Christianity has overcome the apparent tensions between religion and economic action in order to sustain the capitalist economic system. There has been much criticism of Weber's analysis, based on his theory of the Protestant work ethic, of the impact of religion on the rise of capitalism. However, because of the influence of his thesis on subsequent research, I shall attempt to summarise it.

Weber was struck by the fact that the Protestant reformation seemed to give rise to a series of motivations which acted as catalysts in the rise of capitalism. Through emphasising the 'calling' to work as a way of serving God, through warning against the pursuit of frivolous leisure-time activities, and through approving the abolition of laws against usury, the Calvinist work ethic facilitated the accumulation of wealth.

By breaking down the ethical disapproval of traditional capitalism and actively encouraging a methodical approach to economic affairs, Weber argued that proponents of the Protestant work ethic had played a critical role in shaping the economic and social history of Western Europe. According to him, religion determined the economic ethics of individuals. By carrying out their commercial activities in a particular way, people of specific faiths earned a 'premium' on what they were doing.

One of the most controversial aspects of Weber's thesis is his emphasis on Protestantism at the expense of Catholicism. As Trevor-Roper and Little have noted, he used the distinction between Calvinism and Catholicism to explain the spread of capitalism in certain geographical regions, but failed to recognise that some of the earliest centres of capitalism were Catholic cities such as Liege, Lille and Turin. Many of the first capitalist families in Europe were Catholics, Jews and freethinkers – or, in my opinion, the Muslims of Moorish Spain.

This is a good point at which to note what Catholicism has to say on the matter. I have explored the relationship between Catholicism and economics in great detail in *Globalisation for the Common Good* so will only briefly revisit the topic here, then will shed some light on the works of Archbishop William Temple (demonstrating my ecumenism) and briefly summarise the contributions of Judaism and Islam (demonstrating my commiment to interfaith dialogue). I write with an awareness of the ecumenical nature of today's religious dialogue, and the desire of all people of goodwill to learn how to build a society that is just, free and prosperous.

Catholic social teaching is perhaps the richest modern tradition in the field, built upon a century of papal pronouncements. By the late nineteenth century, momentous changes had been brought about as a result of the

Industrial Revolution. In an attempt to bring the insights of transcendent faith to bear on worldly matters, Pope Leo XIII, whose papacy lasted from 1878 to 1903, penned an encyclical letter that became known as the Magna Carta of Catholic social teaching. The revolutionary changes he had witnessed had transformed the social and technological patterns of European life and were the immediate occasion for his *Rerum Novarum* (*Of Revolutionary Change*) in May 1891.

Catholic social teaching is dynamic – always subject to development. In honour of the centenary of Leo XIII's encyclical, Pope John Paul II declared 1991 a Year of Church Social Teaching and issued a ground-breaking new encyclical, *Centesimus Annus* (*The Hundredth Year*), which represented a dramatic development in the encyclical tradition, promoting a just, fair and free economy.

Encyclicals, papal letters circulated throughout the whole of the Catholic Church, have in more recent years been intended to reach beyond the Church to all people of goodwill. As encyclicals, *Rerum Novarum* and *Centesimus Annus* therefore enjoy a privileged position within the hierarchy of official Catholic teaching. The purpose of my brief outline is not to examine the function of Catholic dogmatic teaching but to explore these two instances of Church teaching on social issues.

It is the present pope, John Paul II, who offered a definition of the concept of 'the social teaching of the Church' when, in *Sollicitudo Rei Socialis* (*Social Concern*), published on 30th December, 1987, he stated that it is a 'doctrinal corpus' edited by the magisterium of the Roman Pontiff, beginning with *Rerum Novarum*. In paragraph 44 he explains:

The Church's social doctrine is not a 'third way' between *liberal capitalism* and *Marxist collectivism*, nor even a possible alternative to other solutions less radically opposed to one another: rather, it constitutes a *category of its own*. Nor is it an *ideology*, but rather the *accurate formulation* of the results of a careful reflection on the complex realities of human existence, in society and in the

international order, in the light of faith and of the Church's
tradition. Its main aim is to *interpret* these realities, determining
their conformity with or divergence from the lines of the Gospel
teaching on man and his vocation, a vocation which is at once
earthly and transcendent; its aim is thus to *guide* Christian
behaviour. It therefore belongs to the field, not of *ideology*, but
of *theology* and particularly of moral theology.

He is following closely the definition given in *Gaudium
et Spes* (*The Church in the Modern World*) of 'the duty of scrutinising the signs of the times and of interpreting them in
the light of the Gospel'. As a permanent 'learning process',
the social teaching of the Church should be considered the
result of a dialogue between the magisterium of the pope,
the bishops (whose views are expressed in general and
regional synods and at bishops' conferences), specialists in
social ethics and social sciences, and the people of God. Paul
VI, in *Octogesimo Adveniens*, expressed a methodological
option to this 'learning process':

In the face of such widely varying situations it is difficult for us
to utter a unified message and to put forward a solution which
has universal validity. Such is not our ambition, nor is it our
mission. It is up to the Christian communities to analyze with
objectivity the situation which is proper to their own country, to
shed on it the light of the gospel's unalterable words and to draw
principles of the church... It is up to these Christian communities, with the help of the Holy Spirit, in communion with the
bishops who hold responsibility and in dialogue with other
Christian brethren and all men of good will, to discern the
options and commitments which are called for in order to bring
about the social, political and economic changes seen in many
cases to be urgently needed.

If we start our celebration of one hundred years of
Catholic social thought with the publication of *Rerum
Novarum* (in May 1891), we can pinpoint stages of development in the social teaching of the Church. The earlier pastoral metaphor of the flock and shepherd changed during

the Leonine period (1878-1958) to a view of self and society not limited to the exigencies of life in a sheepfold but seen as part of universal nature, of natural law. This was the period of 'social doctrine' according to Leo XIII, Pius XI and Pius XII, all of it natural-law based: the Magisterium of the Pope provided the only legitimate interpretation. The method was deductive, emphasis being placed on the continuing importance of the principle of subsidiarity as enunciated in *Quadragesimo Anno* (1931).

With John XXIII and Vatican II a turning point was reached: the teaching became more personal, more concrete than in the time of the natural-law approach. An inductive method of see, judge and act was followed in scrutinising the signs of the times and interpreting them in the light of the Gospels. More biblical elements entered into the social teaching of the Church. Drawing on the balanced rationalism of Thomism and *Rerum Novarum*, the Church sought to restore the social order and distributive justice.

Forty years later, the signs of the times were different. The optimism of the late nineteenth century died early in the new century: the First World War was its graveyard. Capitalism faltered and the great depression followed. Fascism and Communism both gained ground. So *Quadragesimo Anno* was radical: it called for reconstruction, not reform. Its keynote was social justice:

[Thus] the statements of the ecclesiastical magisterium furnish us with a precise description of the extent of social justice as the general norm of the life of the entire social body. It is not to be reduced to particular forms of justice, which have to do with the direct relationships between individuals, nor with those which concern the political activities of governors. It includes these different forms: it concerns the dealings of men with one another, inasmuch as they are related to the whole society and its common good, and also the dealings of rulers with ruled, inasmuch as the ruled receive from society their part of the common good. The concept of the common good is at the centre of its definition, and the idea of a social body, of a social universal, really existing by itself, contrary to all nominalist or individualist theory, is implicit in the descriptions which the popes give of social justice.

Although Pius XII was influenced by the fundamental changes in economic theory initiated by Keynes, it was not until Pope John XXIII in 1961 published *Mater et Magistra* (*Mother and Teacher*) that a new methodology and the identification of the problem of 'development' emerged, requiring substantial changes in the social teaching of the Church which were expressed in *Pacem in Terris* (*Peace throughout the World*) in 1963.

The Second Vatican Council, with its Pastoral Constitution *Gaudium et Spes* (1965), moved the Church away from a 'liberal agenda' towards third-world concerns. Its underlying anthropology of social personalism radicalised property ethics.

Paul VI continued these themes, making the transition from 'development' to 'liberation.' His encyclical *Populorum Progressio* (1967) shows the influence of new theories of liberation and sharply criticises capitalism. Paragraph 31 spells out the problem of the justification for revolution:

We know, however, that a revolutionary uprising – save where there is manifest, longstanding tyranny which would do great damage to fundamental personal rights and dangerous harm to the common good of the country – produces new injustices, throws more elements out of balance and brings on new disasters. A real evil should not be fought against at the cost of greater misery.

It hardly justifies capitalism as we know and experience it. Father Philip Land, SJ, lists nine axioms, drawn from the teachings, for judging any economy:

1 The economy is for people;
2 The economy is for being, not having;
3 The economic system ought to be needs-based;

4 The economy is an act of stewardship;
5 The economy must be a participatory society;
6 There must be fair sharing;
7 The system must permit self reliance;
8 The economy must be ecologically sustainable;
9 The economy must be productive.

As John Coleman has noted, Catholic social teaching, as far as it relates to the economy, adheres to the following seven principles:

1 The life and dignity of the human person;
2 The call to family, community and participation;
3 Right and responsibility;
4 The option for the poor and vulnerable;
5 The dignity of work and the rights of workers;
6 Solidarity;
7 Care for God's creation.

I will now turn my attention to providing a brief summary of the Anglican position on economic issues. In the earlier part of the twentieth century the link between Church and State in England meant that there was a clear place for the social teachings and activities of the Church. The possibility of social transformation was seen to depend on finding God in each individual through the communal rituals of worship and service. A wide range of views about economics has been expressed by contemporary Anglicans.

One of the most influential was William Temple, Archbishop of Canterbury from 1942 to 1944. He was a philosopher of religion, an interpreter of Christianity for the general public, who argued from Christian principles and attempted to find solutions to contemporary socioeconomic problems. He greatly influenced the Christian Church through his initiatives in interdenominational and international Church affairs. A man of world stature, Temple was a major influence on the formation of the British Council of Churches and the World Council of

Churches. His theology has been described as a Hegelian idealism, one that combines the interests of Church and State, empowering the Church to make pronouncements on social problems and economic policies.

His many published works include the philosophical essay 'Mens Creatrix' ('The Creative Mind', 1917) and the Gifford Lectures, *Nature, Man and God* (1934), *Christianity and Social Order* (1942) and *The Church Looks Forward* (1944). His strong sense of social responsibility led him to join the Labour Party (1918-25), and he was the first President of the Workers' Educational Association (1908-24) and was also involved with the Student Christian Movement.

He was Chairman of an international interdenominational Conference on Christian Politics, Economics and Citizenship in 1924. He was an Anglican delegate to the ecumenical Faith and Order Conference in 1927, which sought the reunion of the Christian churches, and its chairman in 1937. Concerned with the political responsibilities of being a Christian, he helped organise the Malvern Conference on Church-State relations (1940-41) and used his influence in Parliament to support the Education Act of 1944. As Archbishop of Canterbury, he helped draft a statement to guide the settlement of World War II.

All of his writings reflected his interest in socio-economic issues, but particularly his book *Christianity and the Social Order*. Here he remarks that:

The claim of the Christian Church to make its voice heard in matters of politics and economics is very widely resented, even by those who are Christian in personal belief and in devotional practice. It is commonly assumed that Religion is one department of life, like Art or Science, and that it is playing the part of a busybody when it lays down principles for the guidance of other departments ... This rapid survey of history shows that the claim of the Church to-day to be heard in relation to political and economic problems is no new usurpation, but a reassertion of a right once universally admitted and widely regarded ... The approach to the problem in our own time is to be made along four distinct lines: (1) the claims of sympathy for those who suffer; (2) the educational influence of the social and economic system; (3) the challenge offered to our existing system in the name of justice; (4) the duty of conformity to the 'Natural Order' in which is to be found the purpose of God...

How should the Church interfere? ... Nine-tenths of the work of the Church in the world is done by Christian people fulfilling responsibilities and performing tasks which in themselves are not part of the official system of the Church at all.

... It is of crucial importance that the Church acting corporately should not commit itself to any particular policy... This refusal to adopt a particular policy is partly a matter of prudence ... still more is it a matter of justice, for even though a large majority of Christians hold a particular view, the dissentient minority may well be equally loyal to Christ and equally entitled to be recognised as loyal members of His Church... The Church is committed to the everlasting Gospel and to the Creeds which formulate it; it must never commit itself to an ephemeral programme of detailed action. But this repudiation of direct political action does not exhaust its political responsibility. It must explicitly call upon its members to exercise their citizenship in a Christian spirit... So we answer the question 'How should the Church interfere?' by saying: In three ways – (1) its members must fulfil their moral responsibilities and functions in a Christian spirit; (2) its members must exercise their purely civic rights in a Christian spirit; (3) it must itself supply them with a systematic statement of principles to aid them in doing these two things, and this will carry with it a denunciation of customs or institutions in contemporary life and practice which offend against those principles...

The Church must announce Christian principles and point out where the existing social order at any time is in conflict with them. It must then pass on to Christian citizens, acting in their civic capacity, the task of re-shaping the existing order in closer conformity to the principles... It is sometimes supposed that what the Church has to do is to sketch a perfect social order and urge men to establish it. But it is very difficult to know what a 'perfect social order' means. Is it the order that would work best if we were all perfect? Or is it the order that would work best in a world of men and women such as we actually are?

If it is the former, it certainly ought not to be established; we should wreck it in a fortnight. If it is the latter, there is no reason for expecting the Church to know what it is.... But this task of drawing all men to Himself, the divine purpose to 'sum up all things in Christ', will not be effected till the end of history; and the fellowship of love which it is the divine plan to establish cannot come into being in its completeness within history at all, for it must be more than a fellowship of contemporaries.

The Kingdom of God is a reality here and now, but can be perfect only in the eternal order... The primary principle of Christian Ethics and Christian Politics must be respect for every person simply as a person... The person is primary, not the society; the State exists for the citizen, not the citizen for the State... Freedom is the goal of politics... Freedom, Fellowship, Service – these are the three principles of a Christian social order, derived from the more fundamental Christian postulates that Man is a child of God and is destined for a life of eternal fellowship with Him... Love ... finds its primary expression through Justice – which in the field of industrial disputes means in practice that each side should state its own case as strongly as possibly it can before the most impartial tribunal available...

These two great principles, then – Love and Justice – must be rather regulative of our application of other principles than taken as immediate guides to social policy ... It can all be summed up in a phrase: *the aim of a Christian social order is the fullest possible development of individual personality in the widest and deepest possible fellowship.*

I turn now to the Jewish and Islamic traditions and their relationship with economics. The Torah and the Talmud both present a vision of a just society and a just economy. The pages of the Torah resonate with a profound concern for the socially and economically vulnerable in society – the poor, day laborers, orphans and widows, resident aliens, and even the Levites who, unlike members of other tribes, were assigned no parcels of land in Israel. Much of the contemporary appeal of Judaism derives from this high-minded ethical vision.

The words of Rabbi Jonathan Sacks in an interview given to *Religion & Liberty* ring true:

In Judaism, wealth is seen as both a blessing and as a responsibility. The wealthy are expected to share their blessings with others and to be personal role models of social and communal responsibility: *richesse oblige*. To a considerable extent, that is what happened in most Jewish communities at most times, and it is what saved Jews from the decadence associated with affluence. In Judaism, there is a difference between ownership and possession. What we have, we do not own; rather, we hold it as God's trustees. One of the conditions of that trust is that we share what we possess with those in need. Wealth creation goes hand in hand with the alleviation of poverty – just as, in biblical times, landowners were expected to share part of their harvest with the poor. Jewish teaching is best summarised in the famous aphorism of Hillel: 'If I am not for myself, who will be? But if I am only for myself, what am I?' Judaism is personal responsibility allied with social responsibility.

On stewardship, Dr Sacks remarks that:

Stewardship in Judaism means that we are guardians of the world for the sake of future generations. We must not do irreparable environmental damage. We must create civic amenities. We must ensure that every child has the best possible education. We must provide our own children with the vocational training to become self-sufficient, and so on. An ancient rabbinic tradition teaches that, at the dawn of human history, God said to humankind, 'See the beauty of the universe which I have created – and all that I created, I made for you. Be careful, therefore, that you do not harm what I have made, for if you do, there will be no one left to restore what you have destroyed.

In the sphere of economics, as Lawrence Bush and Jeffrey Dekro have commented, this assumption is underlined by the emphasis in Judaism on the stewardship rather than the ownership of wealth. 'The Divine origin of wealth,' writes Meir Tamari, former chief economist in the Office of the Governor of the Bank of Israel, 'is the central principle of Jewish economic philosophy. Since Judaism is a community-oriented rather than an individual-oriented religion, this means that the group at all levels ... is thereby made a partner in each individual's wealth.'

According to Bush and Dekro, reinforcing this sense of stewardship are the Jewish cycles of work/acquisition and rest/restoration – the weekly sabbath, the sabbatical year and the half-century Jubilee Release that are detailed in *Leviticus* 25:1-13. Stewardship is also the principle underlying the Jewish tradition of *tzedakah* or obligatory alms-giving, which acknowledges charity in its highest forms to be a process of social investment that benefits the donor, the recipient and the whole community. The Jewish holiday, prayer and study cycles likewise contain sources for the development of a Torah of Money:

• The *Sh'ma*, the best-known prayer of the Jewish liturgy, which asserts the unity of God and the cosmic significance of our deeds, can be read as a treatise on communally aware, environmentally responsible economics.

• The concepts of *beracha* and *kedusha* that demand that, before eating and performing other deeds, we must consciously affirm a sense of being blessed ('Whoever enjoys the goods of this world without reciting a blessing is like a thief,' declares the Talmud), offer valuable guidance about limiting wasteful consumption.

• The concept of *s'yag l'Torah*, making 'a fence for the Torah' – that is, establishing practices that keep us from violating Torah teachings even unwittingly or under duress – can be taken as a basis for banning nuclear weapons, the dangers of which threaten the very fabric of creation.

Jonathan Sacks has observed:

A sustainable market economy depends on certain values that are not created by the market – among them, trust, integrity, honesty to customers, loyalty to employees, industry, reliability, and so on. Other values, no less important in the long run, are strong families, a passion for education, and a sense of responsibility to the community. The market encourages competition, but this needs to be balanced by habits of cooperation. As many writers have pointed out, in itself, the market tends to erode those values necessary to its own survival. The market is part, but not the whole, of a free society.

I now turn to the Islamic tradition. Islam offers a complete way of life; it provides rules and guidelines that cover every aspect of society. Naturally, a successful economic system is a vital part of a healthy society: the consumption of goods and services, and the facilitation of this by a common medium of exchange, is essential if people are to realise their material and other goals in life.

Islam sets standards, based on justice and practicality, for the establishment of such an economic system. The aim is to prevent the enmity that often divides different socio-economic strata. While money is considered to be one of the most important elements in society, the accumulation of which concerns almost everyone who participates in transactions with others, its position is secondary to the real purpose of human existence, the worship of Allah.

Responding to the question, '*What is the main message of Islamic Economics to humanity?*' Dr M. Umer Chapra, a former professor of economics at the University of Wisconsin, Kentucky and Lexington, and currently a senior advisor at the Islamic Development Bank in Saudi Arabia, remarked:

The main message is that the humanitarian goal of achieving the well-being of all members of the human family cannot be attained by concentrating primarily on the material constituents of well-being and making maximization of wealth the main objective of Economics. It is also necessary to raise the spiritual content of well-being and reduce all the symptoms of anomie, like family disintegration, conflict and tensions, crime, alcoholism, drug addiction and mental illness, all indicating lack of inner happiness and contentment in the life of individuals. The market system as well as central planning have both failed to lead mankind to such an overall well-being. It is therefore, necessary to lay down the contours of a new system which could help optimise human well-being. This is exactly what Islamic Economics is trying to do.

In a long article on Islamic economy, Ayatullah Muhammad Ali Taskhiri observes:

When we study the Islamic economy as a way which Islam prescribes for individual and social behaviour in the economic field and examine Islam's rules in this area, we can conclude that its most important attribute is *social justice*. In this respect, the Islamic economy resembles all other systems that claim to be serving the human being and realizing his social aspirations, but it differs from them in the details of its conception of social justice.

For justice to emerge, three requirements must be met. Firstly, there must be an understanding of the nature of both private and social property. Private property satisfies man's natural desire to possess the results of his efforts and benefit from his business. Public property guarantees that social action enjoys a social product which may be used to satisfy certain needs and make good shortages.

Secondly, there must be a belief in individual economic freedom as a general, ongoing principle which stems from the nature of ownership, but also an acknowledgement of the limits at which this freedom must end. Thus the interests of the individual will be protected (for example a product may be banned because of the physical or moral damage it could do to someone).

Thirdly, the principle of mutual responsibility must be upheld. Islam guarantees a *subsistence* level for every individual in Islamic society – that is the provision of his natural needs. Any government is obliged to provide this basic minimum for all its citizens; not a single needy person must be found in Islamic society. The State must of course be economically capable of doing this.

• It must oblige individuals to take responsibility and accept their duty to provide for the *necessary* needs of others. One of the responsibilities of government is in fact to compel its citizenss to fulfil their obligations, even those which are individual.

• The legal right of *waliy al-amr* (the head of government) to determine the limits of the public domain (*saddu mantaqat al-mubahat*) through legislation gives the government the necessary power.

• Public property and *anfal* (property with no particular owner) designated public property by the government are used to achieve this goal.

• The necessary funds must come from fines and private *mawqufat* (endowments) taken into public ownership, as when the owners of land or goods die without heirs.

• The aim of Islamic legislation is, as Shahid al-Sadr put it, to strengthen the social structure for the realisation of mutual responsibility.

Fourthly, the principle of social balance must be upheld and the class system repudiated in Islamic society. Our third point was the need for a required minimum subsistence provision for all individuals. As far as the maximum is concerned, the following are determining factors:

• The prohibition of *tabdhir* and *israf* [wasting and squandering] in all areas of life.

• The prohibition of actions leading to the misuse of particular properties, and of *lahw* [amusement] and *mujun* [impudence].

• The rejection of social and economic privileges which discriminate between different groups of people, which prevents the emergence of a class system.

If we scrutinise these points and relate them to human nature and conscience we will find that they contain principles in keeping with natural law. The two extremist social systems, capitalism and socialism, need to moderate their positions after colliding with opposing natural factors.

The natural basis for Islamic views is emphasised by authoritative texts or *nusus*. There are *nusus*, for example, that stress the inherent character of private and public property. The Exalted says: *'And the man shall gain nothing but what he strives for.'* (53:39) – which we can interpret as including worldly possessions. Amir al-Mu'minin says: *'This property is indeed neither mine nor yours but it is a collective property of the Muslims ... what is earned by their hands does not belong to any mouths other than, theirs.'* (Nahj al-Balaghah, sermon 232.)

Some *nusus* emphasise natural economic freedom. The clearest of these is the rule upon which all *fuqaha'* (Islamic scholars) rely: people are in control of their property. Naturally there are limits to this freedom, but the restrictions are only for the benefit of individuals and society.

There are *nusus* that emphasise the need for mutual responsibility and co-operation: neglect of this principle is a rejection of *din* (the faith). The Exalted says: *'Have you seen the person who rejects the religion? He is the one who treats the orphan with harshness, and does not urge {others} to feed the poor.'* (107:1-3)

Finally, there are *nusus* that stress the necessity for balance in a society by emphasising the prohibition of *israf* (squandering) and the renunciation of poverty, thus providing subsistence for every individual. The Imam says, speaking of the duties of the *waliy al-amr* (leader) towards the needy subject: 'He keeps giving him from *zakah* till he makes him needless.'

We can see that, in harmony with other religions, Islam teaches social justice. Allah will provide for every person whom He has brought into life. The competition for natural resources that is presumed to exist among the nations of the world is an illusion. While the earth has sufficient bounty to satisfy the needs of mankind, the challenge for us lies in discovering, extracting, processing and distributing these resources to all who need them.

Finally, I would like to draw the attention of the reader to an important but sadly neglected point. Many notable Western economists have in the past been inspired by Islamic scholarship but this has not always been acknowledged. One of the most notable Muslim scholars was Ibn-Khaldun, who gave us a multi-disciplinary, dynamic model of the economy, very different from the neo-classical model which relies primarily on economic variables.

Who was Ibn-Khaldun? His real name was Abd al-Rahman Ibn Mohammad, but he took the name of a remote ancestor. His parents, Yemenite Arabs, settled in Spain but, after the fall of Seville, migrated to Tunisia where he was born in 1332 CE. He received his early education there and, still in his teens, entered the service of the Egyptian ruler Sultan Barquq.

Ibn-Khaldun's chief contribution lies in the philosophy of history and sociology. He sought to write a world history preambled by a first volume analysing historical events. This volume, commonly known as *Muqaddimah* or Prolegomena, was based on Ibn-Khaldun's unique approach and original contribution and is considered a masterpiece in its field. The chief aim of the monumental work was to identify psychological, economic, environmental and social factors that contribute to the progress of human civilisation and the currents of history.

He analysed the dynamics of group relationships and showed how *al-'Asabiyya* (group-feelings) give rise to a new civilisation and political power which, later on, becomes diffused into a more general civilisation which nurtures fresh new *'Asabiyya*. He identified an almost rhythmic repetition of rise and fall in human civilisations, and analysed the factors contributing to it.

Unlike most of the earlier writers who interpreted history largely in a political context, he emphasised the environmental, sociological, psychological and economic factors which governed events. This revolutionised the science of history and laid the foundation for *umraniyat* (sociology).

Ibn-Khaldun's influence on history, sociology, political science and education is huge. His books have been translated into many languages, in both East and West, and continue to influence the development of these sciences. Dr Ibrahim Oweiss, professor of economics at Georgetown University, calls him the true 'father of economics':

His significant contributions to economics, however, should place him in the history of economic thought as a major forerunner, if not the 'father,' of economics, a title which has been given to Adam Smith, whose great works were published some three hundred and seventy years after Ibn-Khaldun's death. Not only did Ibn-Khaldun plant the germinating seeds of classical economics, whether in production, supply, or cost, but he also pioneered in consumption, demand, and utility, the cornerstones of modern economic theory.

Oweiss notes that Ibn-Khaldun placed economics within a framework of laws based on religious and moral perceptions for the good of all humanity. All economic activities were to be undertaken in accordance with such laws.

The relationship between moral and religious principles on the one hand and good government on the other is explained in his discussion of the famous letter that Tahir Ibn al-Husayn (775-822) wrote to his son 'Abdallah, who, with his descendants, ruled Khurasan until 872. From the rudimentary thoughts of Tahir he developed a theory of taxation which has influenced modern economic thought, even economic policies in the United States.

Oweiss observes that Ibn-Khaldun had given substance and depth to earlier elemental economic ideas and that centuries later these same ideas were developed by the Mercantilists, the commercial capitalists of the seventeenth century, and others, including Sir William Petty (1623-87), Adam Smith (1723-90), David Ricardo (1772-1823), Thomas R. Malthus (1766-1834), Karl Marx (1818-83) and John Maynard Keynes (1883-1946), and also by contemporary economic theorists.

In conclusion Oweiss remarks:

Even if Adam Smith was not directly exposed to Ibn-Khaldun's economic thoughts, the fact remains that they were the original seeds of classical economics and even modern economic theory. Ibn-Khaldun had not only been well established as the father of the field of sociology, but he had also been well recognised in the field of history, as the following passage from Arnold Toynbee indicates:

> In his chosen field of intellectual activity [Ibn-Khaldun] appears to have been inspired by no predecessors ... and yet, in the Prolegomena ... to his *Universal History* he has conceived and formulated a philosophy of history which is undoubtedly the greatest work of its kind that has yet been created by any mind in any time or place.

Through his great sense and knowledge of history, and his meticulous observation of men, times and places, Ibn-Khaldun produced an original system of economic thought. His was the first wide-ranging and organised contribuion to the subject of economics. He touched on many aspects: value and its relationship to labour; capital accumulation and its effect on the rise and fall of dynasties; the dynamics of demand, supply, prices and profits; money and the role of governments; and expounded his remarkable theory of taxation. His contributions should indeed make Ibn-Khaldun the 'father of economics'.

I hope that this brief summary of Islamic economics, and in particular Ibn-Khaldun, will help to promote the idea of interfaith dialogue, of mutual respect and understanding for other religions. For too long now since 9/11, the promoters of fear of a clash of civilisations have monopolised our thinking in their attempt to degrade, dishonour and dehumanise the Muslim people in general and the Islamic culture and heritage in particular.

CHAPTER 7

Summing Up

BY MARCUS BRAYBROOKE

THE WORD 'university' is in its derivation related to the word 'universe' and suggests wholeness. A university should be a place where human endeavours to understand the universe are brought together. Twentieth-century specialisation, whilst greatly increasing our knowledge, has, however, also fragmented it. As a student of history I quickly learned that, if you asked anything of an expert, the reply would be, 'It's not my period.' Kamran shows how specialisation in economics, with its emphasis on mathematics, has isolated the subject from a wider canvas which asks moral questions about the purpose of economic activity. The study of religions also can become descriptive of rituals or narrowly focussed on sacred texts and also avoid questions of meaning.

It is difficult enough today to keep up in one's own field, let alone master another. Few people are likely to be sufficiently versed in both economics and theology to convince the experts in either field. This is why the effort to relate the two disciplines needs to be collaborative and why a centre where economists and theologians could work alongside each other would be very valuable. Indeed, the search for the common good should also involve people of many other disciplines.

Because the approach needs to be collaborative, we must question the emphasis on competition which, rampant in the business world, has also affected academia. The utopian dream of eliminating competition seems unrealistic. In the

Book of Genesis, after the Fall we are told that God accepted the offerings of Abel, but not of his brother Cain. We are not told why. As we grow up we may wonder why some people are more beautiful or more successful – indeed why some people are born to health and wealth and others to illness and deprivation. Maybe it is our karma. Yet even if we cannot answer the question 'Why?' we learn to live with success and failure. Clearly competition motivates people in many fields of life, such as sport, business and the arts. Referees and lawyers try to ensure that there is no unfair competition, but as yet there has been little success in controlling the worst effects of globalisation.

At best, the role of the law is negative. It aims to stop unfairness and, in the current catchphrase, to ensure 'a level playing field'. Far more important, however, is inner motivation. People need to recognise that there are other and higher values in life than power and wealth. This, as Kamran insists, is why other values besides competition need to be applied to our economic activity. These values, however, do not derive from economics but from the moral and spiritual framework which, above all, has been provided by the great world religions.

The primary task of the religions is to proclaim these values as they are found in the particular context of each religion's teaching and practice, but religious teachers need to work with economists in seeing how these values apply to specific situations. Too easily, the opinions of religious leaders are ignored by politicians and businessmen because to them they seem 'unrealistic'. In part, this may be because politicians and businessmen reject the moral challenge, which is why the call for inner change or transformation is central to the message of each religion, but it may be also that the issue is more complex than religious leaders sometimes recognise.

It may be, moreover, that some politicians and businessmen – and this is true of some religious leaders – assume that their view of life is the only reasonable approach. They have not learned to live in a pluralist world and to listen to others. Indeed one reason there is so much hostility to America in many places is the fear that Americans will tread roughshod over other cultures and ways of seeing the world. It soon became clear, for example, at the meeting of members of the World Bank with faith representatives, that each had a very different understanding of the development they sought. Maximising profit, if it meant the destruction of community life, was for many people of faith an undesirable form of development.

This is why economists and theologians from many cultures and faiths need to engage each other. This dialogue is beginning to happen, but a centre which can promote and highlight this will help to ensure that new insights begin to influence political and business decisions. The danger is that, if an ever larger number of people feel both politically marginalised and economically deprived, then the fissures already apparent in our contemporary world will widen even more, causing untold suffering to millions of people.

It is not too late for a change of heart, which is the message of the great faiths. Only this can ensure that there is a sufficient will to provide at least the basic necessities of life for all people – but only politicians, economists and businessmen who seek the common good can ensure that effective programmes are in place to achieve this.

CHAPTER 8

The Way Forward

BY KAMRAN MOFID

W HILE I WAS gathering my thoughts together for this chapter, a friend drew my attention to an article, 'Religions for Peace' by Michael Amaladoss, SJ, a professor of theology at Vidyajyoti College in Delhi and director of the Institute for Dialogue with Cultures and Religions in Chennai. I was inspired by his eloquent, wise words, so relevant to what I was intending to write:

Religion is the deepest element in human and social life and it deals with ultimate meanings ...

Religion-less economic and political orders were the creation of the Enlightenment. Human reason is seen as the ultimate mentor in everything; every sector is autonomous; economic structures are driven by the pursuit of profit in the context of free trade; political order is a balancing of the interests of various groups in society. Free trade has resulted in a world polarised between rich and poor, internationally and locally. The easy movement of capital around the world has only made the gap wider. Balancing political interests is not a realistic goal in a world dominated by one superpower. All it can hope to achieve is a balancing act between a few rich and powerful nations; it ignores and marginalises the interests of all the other nations on the globe. The continuing arms race and the increasing production and sale of arms are examples of political failure. There is no true participative democracy anywhere, either within or between nations, thanks to the power games of interest groups.

Can any of this lead to lasting peace? I doubt it. For true peace we need a sense of human, moral and spiritual values. We need to recognise and respect the cultural and religious identities of individuals in every community. We need to appreciate the importance of a quest for the common good, both locally and universally, which will lead to justice and equality. I do not believe a secular order is capable of delivering this.

The failure of recent efforts to impose an ecological discipline on the nations of the world is just one example of how things are going wrong. The manipulation of international agencies, mainly by powerful countries, is another. Throughout history, religion has been the only prophetic force to challenge our imperfect efforts at building communities. No religion actually preaches violence: they alone speak of forgiveness and reconciliation.

All the great religions accept the common destiny of human beings and have a positive attitude towards the pluralism of faiths. None encourages interreligious conflict. Buddhism sets no store on particular rituals but proposes a way of meditation for all. Hinduism sees different religions as various ways to spiritual liberation: all rivers run to the sea. Christianity has come to recognise the presence of the Spirit of God in all religions in forms unknown to many. Moslems are enjoined by the Qur'an to respect diversity in religion: 'There must be no coercion in matters of faith' (2:256). God has not made everyone a Muslim and His will must be accepted. People of different religions must be allowed to go their own way: 'Unto you your moral law, and unto me, mine' (109:6). Such openness requires us to respect and accept every person and group as sharing in a common destiny, even if we think that our own way is better. We must exclude no one from God's love and mercy because all are children of one God.

Religions can and should agree on the defence and promotion of common human and spiritual values, even if each religion justifies them in terms of its own principles. Justice and peace are the goals of all religions. Since the Second World War all religions have produced theologies of liberation which seek to promote justice and community.

It is not that we need to establish theocratic states. Economics and politics should remain autonomous, but their autonomy will not be absolute. They need to be responsive to moral values and principles: they need a dialogue with religion.

All religions accept that human beings are imperfect and sinful. Conflicts are inevitable. There will always be a need for forgiveness and reconciliation, for love and compassion for others. Only religions can promote this. Secular reasoning and a balancing of self-interests will not take us that far.

Every crisis is an opportunity. At the present time our world is very troubled, and everyone is saying the struggle is going to be a long one. The challenge is for us to come up with a new world order based on principles of freedom, justice and community inspired by the religions of the world in dialogue. Flushing out and bringing to justice a network of terrorists is not going to bring world peace. It is not even the first step. It is no more than the removal of an irritant. Unless the situation is changed radically, others will simply replace them. The real task is to start building a society based on justice and equality. We need a conversion.

A moment like this brings out the best and the worst in us: courage and generosity, but also all our prejudices – our individual and collective egoism, our narrow nationalism, our sense of hurt pride, our double standards. We need a new vision of humanity and world community and we have to find new ways of empowering people to shape it. This is the only way to achieve true peace in the world.

As Father Amaladoss and others have said, and as I have already noted, economic life was formerly regarded as a branch of the moral life of the whole community; today it has become an amoral zone. We have shaken ourselves free from many forms of tyranny but have achieved just one kind of emancipation; in the process we have delivered ourselves into the hands of a philosophy which has swept away the basis for any common social purpose. Economic activity needs moral regulation. The main problems in the world today are not economic or technological. What is really wrong with modern society is that it is morally sick.

R.H. Tawney described 'acquisitive' societies. The whole preoccupation of our modern way of life is the acquisition of wealth. Rights are divorced from duties; the unrestricted pursuit of self-interest is the ruling ethos. A society of this kind, which has taken off the moral brakes, consists of individuals who see no ends other than their own, no laws other than their own desires and no limits beyond those they set themselves. It sets the individual at the centre of the universe and dissolves moral principles into choices of expediency.

In our materialistic environment there is much emphasis on wealth-creation, but no room for the creator, and no proper relationship between creator and creation. We should not forget that our most important economic resources owe nothing to human labour and ordering, nothing to economic factors in general. The land, the air, the sea, the sun, and vital natural resources such as oil, gas and coal, are all God's gifts: they should be for the benefit of all God's creation.

Aggression, selfishness and greed, disrespect for the common good, have made a mockery of that. Modern economic theory, which lacks any true religious foundation, has created its own god, the god of Mammon. It has degraded God's creation in the name of economic progress. What a bitter harvest this has become!

If we could align the most powerful force in capitalism, namely wealth-creation, with ethical objectives, by bringing economics and theology together, then the world would be a better, safer place, and globalisation could become a force for good. If only we could link theology and economics we could make the study of these subjects far more effective than if they continue to be analysed in isolation. We should not reject the imperatives of economics, politics and trade *per se* but should apply them to the common good: everybody must become a stakeholder; everybody must benefit.

My argument is that it is only by bringing together the common beliefs within our religious traditions and applying them to our economic systems that we can create an all-inclusive world for the good of everyone. As Hans Küng stresses, ethics should be firmly rooted in religion, otherwise there is no binding force. Only religions can speak with one voice on ethical issues, covering all aspects of respect for life.

Why should we try to combine religion and economics? Because they have a common end: that all may live happily. It is proper that they should employ different methods in order to achieve this end. One uses the production and exchange of goods and services, the other selfless service, love and compassion. Religions could – if they will speak with their original source of inspiration – greatly contribute towards restoring the balance between the material and the spiritual elements and thus show the way to live fully human lives in a peaceful, just and sustainable society.

The ethical and spiritual teachings of all religions and their striving for the common good can provide us with a clear and focused model of moral behaviour in what we term 'the marketplace'. An overall ethical orientation to the challenges of daily economic activity can be related to each of our faith traditions. In the Jewish tradition we see the effort to balance pragmatic considerations of economic efficiency with ideals of interpersonal equity and social justice. The key themes of Christian and Islamic thought are, respectively, a concern for human dignity and a concern for communal solidarity. These three themes are not separate: they overlap and interlock; and they are shared by all three traditions. Together they form an inspiring mosaic of Western religious ethics.

The traditions of the East have somewhat different themes from those of the Abrahamic religions; nonetheless, there is much that is similar. The importance of humility and patience characterises the Hindu view of economic life. In Buddhism, the theme that resonates most strongly is compassion; in Confucian thought it is reciprocity. These, also, are not separate themes, but overlapping and interlocked. The mosaic they form is not sharply distinct from that of the Western traditions. Related to the marketplace, it would inspire businessmen to exhibit mutual compassion, while individual achievement would not be at the expense of communal solidarity. Steady economic and moral improvement would be pursued with humility and patience. In all, these must become the guiding principles, the vision behind the teachings of a new economics: the marketplace is not just an economic sphere, 'it is a region of the human spirit'.

I should like to make four appeals: firstly to my fellow economists, secondly to our religious leaders, thirdly to our business community, and fourthly to the global financial and trade establishment.

To my fellow economists. If you truly want to change the world for the better, you should grasp the nettle and explore the relevance of ethics, morality, spirituality and religion to the functioning of the economy and globalisation. As long as our subject is trapped within the narrow confines of individualism, self-interest, greed and profit maximisation, we cannot heal our broken world. 'Each man for himself and the devil take the hindmost' has turned our discipline into a 'dismal' science. By going back to our roots, by bringing economics closer to theology and ethics, we can, once again, make economics a subject 'of harmony and beauty, all its parts co-operating for the common good, and its inbuilt laws distributing benefits equitably'. Please come on board. If there is a department of theology at your university, then establish a working relationship with it. Arrange meetings and joint seminars; encourage students to take electives from the department of theology. And why don't you yourself take a course in theology? You will find it inspiring.

To our religious leaders. Now more than ever before you are called upon to speak out on global issues, on matters relating to economics and globalisation. Clergymen and women can undoubtedly play a vital role in urging that religious ethics be brought to bear on economic decision-making, but changes in their training are needed if they are to start to be effective in that role. Just as the market-place needs a better understanding of religious ethics, so do our clerics need a better understanding of the reality of the marketplace. They need to become engaged in the kinds of dialogues I have urged on the economists and to do this they need to study economics – but not *any* sort of economics. Most of what is taught at our universities is neo-liberalism – and this is precisely what should be avoided.

To our business leaders. In this age of globalisation you are in a unique position to influence society for years to come. With this power comes monumental responsibility. You can choose to ignore this responsibility, and thereby exacerbate problems such as economic inequality, environmental degradation and social injustice, but this will compromise your ability to do business in the long run. The world of good business needs a peaceful and just world in which to operate and prosper.

To the global financial and trade establishment. We all share a deep concern for the poor and marginalised and are all responsible for promoting the common good, alleviating poverty and preserving the natural environment, and we need to acknowledge that true progress must be more than economic progress. As R.H.Tawey in *Religion and the Rise of Capitalism* wisely observed:

A reasonable estimate of economic organisation must allow for the fact that, unless industry is to be paralysed by recurrent revolts on the part of outraged human nature, it must satisfy criteria which are not purely economic.

The World Bank, IMF and WTO, with other financial and trade institutions, greatly influence the way the global economy operates, and thus the quality of our lives. Nearly all of their proposals on the global economy concern the need to unleash the power of the market, liberalise trade, deregulate and privatise – which are purely economic considerations. It is as though humanity and the environment are irrelevant except as servants of the overarching need to expand the global economy – as if that could satisfy all human needs and aspirations.

However, the Human Development Report 2004, *Cultural Liberty in Today's Diverse World*, makes it clear that many other issues are important for human well-being:

Accommodating people's growing demands for their inclusion in society, for respect of their ethnicity, religion, and language, takes more than democracy and equitable growth. Also needed are multicultural policies that recognize differences, champion diversity and promote cultural freedoms, so that all people can choose to speak their language, practice their religion, and participate in shaping their culture – so that all people can choose to be who they are.

Why can such considerations not inform the deliberations and proposals of the World Bank, IMF and WTO? Economics, commerce and trade, without a true understanding of the aspirations of the people it is affecting, cannot bring justice and peace to all. Social transformation can be achieved only when unselfish love, spirituality and a rigorous pursuit of justice are embraced.

Which is why I have argued that economists need to engage in dialogue with theologians to deepen their understanding of ethical and moral issues. A similar engagement of financial and trade institutions with religious organisations would enhance this process but, as far as I know, there has not yet been any such dialogue. At the meetings of the World Economic Forum in Davos there has been some participation by religious organisations, but the value of such engagements remains to be assessed.

More obviously helpful has been the establishment of the World Faiths Development Dialogue (WFDD) in 1998 by James D. Wolfensohn, President of the World Bank, and Lord Carey, then Archbishop of Canterbury, for the promotion of a dialogue on poverty and development among the different faith traditions and between them and development agencies such as the World Bank.

This is a positive step, and it is recognised by both parties that, while religion uses the standard of distribution and equity to evaluate economic policy and economics uses the standard of production and efficiency, it does not require a trade-off between efficiency and equity to create a better world. As Archbishop William Temple in *Christianity and Social Order* observed, 'The art of government in fact is the art of so ordering life that self-interest prompts what justice demands'.

A further example of the co-operation of the World Bank with faith communities has been its helping to establish the Alliance of Religions and Conservation (ARC) in 1995. The Bank is still one of its main sponsors and has agreed to work alongside major faith groups to develop alternative models of economic and ecological progress.

As the World Bank has expressed such a serious desire to engage with faith communities, I would like to encourage both parties to work closely together with the International Finance Corporation (IFC) which is engaged in many projects in developing countries. As explained on its website (www.ifc.org), the IFC, which has its headquarters in Washington, DC, is a member of the World Bank Group and shares the primary objective of all their institutions: to improve the quality of the lives of people in its developing member countries. The President of the World Bank Group, James D. Wolfensohn is also IFC president.

The website notes, '*The world was a different place 40 years ago.*' No talk of emerging markets, no worldwide trend towards privatization, no communications revolution, no globalized economy. World population was less than half of what it is today. The economies of poor countries were in the very early stages of development, lacking the human resources, physical infrastructure and sound institutions needed to raise incomes and improve living standards. The responsibility for development was almost universally assigned to the public sector. Private-sector investment was small and little thought was given to increasing it.

For several years the World Bank had supported the creation of a new institution to complement their own. They had been founded to finance post-World War II reconstruction and development projects by lending money to member governments – and this they had been doing very effectively. Yet early on some of their senior staff had seen the need for a sister institution to encourage greater private-sector investment in poor countries.

Multinational corporations and commercial financial institutions at the time showed little interest in investing in Africa, Asia, Latin America or the Middle East and entrepreneurs in these regions had few domestic sources of capital. A catalyst was needed. It was into this environment that the IFC was born in 1956.

According to one of the founding fathers, Robert L. Garner, former US banker and General Foods Corporation executive, an ardent believer in private enterprise, it was entrepreneurship that would bring prosperity to developing countries – 'that elusive combination of the imagination to see an opportunity and to mobilize the necessary resources to seize it'. What was also needed was capital from private investors willing to take substantial risks in return for potentially large rewards. Other needs were seen to be job-creation projects, training towards new labour and management skills and technological advances. In the process business owners in developing countries would 'successfully transmute machines, labour and capital into a dynamic going concern, producing at competitive cost goods of a quality that the market will accept'. These new businesses would be important new tools to help developing countries reduce poverty and build solid futures.

And all these wonderful things would result from economic growth, from the creation of a sound economic and commercial environment. I find it disheartening that there is no serious reference to the encouragement of humane policies leading to justice and peace for all. The website is strong on economics but reticent about the need for compassion and respect for other ideas and civilisations. Again, there is a bullying 'one size fits all' philosophy

This misunderstanding of the world and its peoples is very destructive. Under James Wolfensohn the World Bank has been showing a different kinf of leadership but they must take note if they truly wish to bring development with justice to the world.

As this book is being launched in Kenya, a pertinent question for the World Bank and the IFC is: 'Given what Robert Garner envisaged, and given that Kenya signed the Article of Agreement with the IFC in 1964 – forty-one years ago – what has so drastically gone wrong?'

The answer is not difficult. Concentrating on wealth-creation and economic growth alone is wrong. While wealth is vitally important, it needs to be created for a noble reason. Economic growth must have a spirit and there must also be the creation of justice and peace for all the community, of which the entrepreneur is a member.

That is why I am inviting the World Bank to bring the IFC and the faith communities together, so that each can have a positive impact on the other. Then perhaps we can have both efficiency and equity, economic growth and social justice, rights for the individual and for the community. Perhaps a way could be found to manage economic and ethical values as if they were one and the same.

Lord Carey, James Wolfensohn, the Secretary General of ARC, Martin Palmer, and others already involved in this sort of dialogue with the World Bank should be commended, but it still faces serious resistance. There are both opportunities and pitfalls.

Other financial and trade organisations need to emulate the good example of the World Bank, but for this to happen we must have economists and theologians who understand each other well enough to work together. *I cannot overstress the need for such dialogue.* The world would be a better place as a result – we could provide humane solutions to problems of efficiency and productivity, equality and social justice, rights and responsibilities in the process of globalisation.

At this critical point in global history our business leaders and financial institutions, alongside representatives of the world's religions, face a daunting challenge and an inspiring opportunity. Their joint strengths and assets are immense and could be used to pursue issues of pivotal significance to their communities and the whole world.

The ethical and spiritual teachings of all religions, their common striving for the common good, can provide a clear and focused model of moral behaviour in the marketplace. Religious and commercial ideals such as fairness, solidarity, patience, service and compassion, as well as efficiency and profit, should combine to lead us to create an equitable and united world. The marketplace is much more than just an economic sphere.

In calling for this dialogue, I appeal to the deep instinctive understanding of the common good that all people share – to our essential humanity. We have to deal with the most pressing concerns of people the world over. Religion has always been a major factor in the growth of human civilisation; but commerce and wealth-creation, when undertaken for noble reasons, are also vital for human survival. The challenge is to get the two to work together to bring about economic justice and opportunities for all God's people.

The challenge cannot be delayed or avoided, so what should be done? We need to encourage both the reading and the writing of works on economics and globalisation for the common good and it should become a compulsory subject of study in university departments of economics, business and theology, as well as in seminaries. A further step, because education has such an important role to play in deepening our understanding of legitimate human aspirations and how these may be accommodated in a just social order, a centre dedicated to the promotion of this vision for our world needs to be, and hopefully will be, established. I hope that, in this presentation, I have shown how all these things, and more, may come about.

Finally, I have already touched on the pivotal role of love in taking us to the Promised Land but I would like to end my journey by shedding more light on this revelation.

One of the most serious consequences of neo-liberal economic theory, which measures everything in materialistic terms, judging it worthwhile only if it is of monetary value or able to create wealth, is our loss of innocence, and of intimacy. We are not given the opportunity of discovering 'the art of loving'.

My inspiration for these thoughts are the excellent writings of Erich Fromm, and in particular his memorable book *The Art of Loving*. He was a German psychoanalyst and social philosopher who fled his homeland when the Nazis came to power, settling in the United States. There he combined clinical practice and lecturing at Columbia University.

Most of his early writings were about how totalitarian regimes come to be accepted and supported by the people. In *The Fear of Freedom* he argued that such regimes appeal to a deep-seated craving to escape from the freedom of the modern world and return to the womb. But Fromm had no illusions about the society to which he had emigrated. He was among the first to see that twentieth-century capitalist democracies offered another form of escape from freedom. In *The Sane Society* he developed ideas from Freud's *Civilisation and its Discontents*, arguing that capitalist society, where 'consumption has become the de facto goal', was itself sick.

In *The Art of Loving* Fromm quotes, among others, Huxley and Rumi to hammer home his points. He identifies five types of love, all of them under threat. Brotherly love ('which underlies all others') has been undermined by the commodification of human beings. Motherly love is threatened by narcissism and possessiveness. Self-love (without which we cannot love others) is corrupted by selfishness. The love of God is regressing 'to an idolatric concept of God'. Erotic love has been debased by its separation from brotherly love and the absence of tenderness. Fromm questioned whether 'the social structure of Western civilisation and the spirit arising from it are conducive to the development of love' and concluded that 'to raise the question is to answer it in the negative'.

The world today is a market, says Fromm: our whole culture is based on the idea of 'mutually favourable exchange'. This concept includes our assessement of people. 'Attractive' usually means a nice package of qualities which are popular and sought-after on the 'personality market' – which is largely a Hollywood construct.

Two persons thus fall in love when they feel they have found the best object available on the market, considering the limitations of their own exchange values. In a culture in which the marketing orientation prevails, and in which material success is the outstanding value, there is little reason to be surprised that human relations follow the same pattern of exchange which governs the commodity and labour market.

Fromm wrote *The Art of Loving* at a time when capitalism was relatively benign and regulated. Fifty years on, our contemporary world driven by a supercharged and unregulated global market economy confirms his statement that 'a healthy economy is possible only at the price of unhealthy human beings'. In the past decade in many Western capitalist economies we have achieved the lowest rates of interest, inflation and unemployment for forty years, and unprecedented growth. Yet mental health has declined sharply. More than two million Britons are on antidepressants, half a million are on Class A drugs. Binge drinking, and what Fromm called 'acts of destruction' (violence, vandalism and self-abuse) have reached record levels. This could be called the age of progress and poverty: we are economically rich but poor in spirit and happiness.

Neil Clark, writing in *New Statesman*, has noted:

'... while Fromm's five types of love continue to decline, forms of pseudo-love abound. What Fromm called '*egoisme a deux*', in which two self-centred people come together in marriage or partnership to escape loneliness, but never arrive at a 'central relationship', is clearly thriving in a country where more than a third of cohabiting and married couples keep separate bank accounts. Narcissism, which Fromm said we had to overcome if we were ever to achieve true love, is everywhere: when we switch on the television, open a tabloid newspaper or overhear casual conversation in the street or on a bus.

Given what is happening all around us, we should be able to see that

... a society that is driven by rapacious commercialism, which lauds and promotes the cult of self, and which quantifies success in purely material terms, will always produce less love and therefore more unhappy people than one which places human needs first. Global capitalism does many things, but building solidarity is not among them.

Here again we can be inspired by the wisdom of our religions if we note what they say about love and its true meaning and value.

The major religions of the world prescribe the unselfish love and service of others. Only when this love is extended to all humanity without exception will a dignified and peaceful human future become possible. The Hindu faith states that in service to others is happiness; in selfishness is misery and pain. For the Sikhs, God is love and love is God. St Paul wrote, 'Love (*agape*) is patient, love is kind. It does not envy, it does not boast, it is not proud. It is not rude, it is not self-seeking, it is not easily angered, it keeps no records of wrongs' (I *Corinthians* 13). Buddhism teaches us to cultivate universal compassion. Judaism teaches that 'those who are kind reward themselves' (*Proverbs* 11:17). The Qur'an reads, 'My mercy and compassion embrace all things' (7:156). In these and in other traditions, unselfish love is deemed to be a creative presence underlying, and integral with, all reality, participation in which constitutes the fullest experience of spirituality.

There is an urgent need to realise unselfish love in our increasingly globalised world. Love is a joyful and whole-hearted concern with the well-being of others that can be expressed as tolerance and forgiveness, or as compassion and care, as service to the neediest as well as the nearest. When we extend ourselves to others in this way we become happier and more content; paradoxically, in the giving of self lies the unsought discovery of self. If we desire to realise a globalisation which is good for all, we must remember that social transformation can occur only when unselfish love, spiritual experience and a rigorous pursuit of justice are linked together.

My Response to Marcus Braybrooke

I FIRST MET Marcus a few months before the first conference on interfaith and globalisation which I convened
in Oxford in July 2002, though I already knew him well
through his publications. His wonderful writings on different aspects of interfaith dialogue were a source of inspiration to me. Since then we have been travelling together
on our quest for the common good. Marcus, and indeed
the other two leading religious personalities associated with
this book, care deeply and passionately about moral and
ethical values. I am a blessed man for knowing them the
way I do.

My dialogue with Marcus while preparing this book
reminded me what an important role clergymen and
women can play in urging that religious ethics be brought
to bear on economic decision-making. I was encouraged
that he also felt that our religious leaders ought to encourage changes in theological training that would make it
multi-disciplinary.

In our discussions Marcus quoted the Anglican theologian F.D. Maurice, who remarked that his job was 'to dig,
to show that economy and politics have a ground beneath
themselves, that society is not to be made anew by arrangements of ours, but it is to be regenerated by finding the
law and ground of its order and harmony and the only
secret of its existence in God'. I enjoyed this quotation and
was encouraged to dig deeper for knowledge. Some gems
I discovered are presented in my section on personalities
from different faiths.

Marcus and I agreed that, although increased productivity, efficiency and production of wealth are important
elements of a functional economy, so is the equitable distribution of that wealth. If a successful economy cannot
ensure the latter, it is a social organisation that has failed
to achieve its proper end. We agreed that the goal of the

economic process should be to aid the development and the perfection of human personality, dignity and happiness. This can occur only within a social community which cultivates the virtue of justice and consideration for the common good.

Religions, which represent one of the oldest and most enduring global networks, rooted in strong ethical principles not currently dominant within the global market, must, we both felt, be able to offer insights into ways of redirecting the global economy towards the common good. Put simply, religions use the standard of distribution or equality to evaluate economic policy; economics uses the standard of production and efficiency. We agreed that, to create a better world, a way must be found to advance both sets of values together. For just and wise policies to emerge, the area of their convergence must be increased.

A further source of joy in my debate with Marcus has been to discover how focused he is on his interfaith work. His belief is that the more deeply committed we are to our own faith, the greater our reverence for the faiths of other people; by sharing our convictions, each of us grows in our appreciation of the Divine Mystery. Religious exclusivism and claims to uniqeness inhibit open dialogue and co-operation. I wholeheartedly agree. In an age in which the world is becoming a global village one needs to be increasingly aware of the 'other'. But first we must become more aware of ourselves, and how our destiny is intertwined with that of others.

Marcus and I agreed that there is a great need to address these issues. Ministers of all faiths need to broaden their theological horizons if they are to offer helpful moral, ethical and spiritual guidance. A serious study of other religions must become a core subject at religious seminaries. Sadly this is not the case yet. Religious leaders are today, more than ever before, being called upon to participate at economic forums. How can they be effective participants if their theological training lets them down?

This is why Marcus and I also agree that economics – but not *any* economics – should be a core module in seminaries. To this end we strongly believe in the need for a centre in which the worlds of economics and theology can be brought together, to ensure that new insights begin to influence political and economic decisions. A multicultural world needs an interfaith, multi-discipline centre to promote 'Rekindling the Human Spirit and Compassion in Globalisation'. It would demand compassionate solutions to the challenges of globalisation and seek to promote justice and peace for all God's people.

It is my sincere hope that the dialogue presented in this book will go a long way towards the realisation of this shared dream.

SOURCES CONSULTED

Alves, Ruben, *A Theology of Human Hope*, Abbey Press, St Meinrad, Ind, 1975.

Amaladoss, Michael SJ, 'Religions for Peace', www.newpeoplemedia.org.

Andelson, Robert (ed), *Commons Without Tragedy: Protecting the Environment from Overpopulation*, Shepheard-Walwyn, London, and Barnes & Noble, Savage, Maryland, 1991.

Andelson, Robert & James Dawsey, *From Wasteland to Promised Land: Liberation Theology for a Post-Marxist World*, Shepheard-Walwyn, London, and Orbis Books, Maryknoll, NY, 1992.

Aquinas, Thomas (trans C.I. Litzinger OP), *Commentary on Aristotle's* Nicomachean Ethics, Dumb Ox Books, Notre Dame, 1993.

Aristotle (trans Davis Ross), *Nicomachean Ethics*, Oxford University Press, Oxford, 1980.

Atherton, John (ed), *Social Christianity: A Reader*, SPCK, London, 1994.

Augustine, St (trans G.E. McCracken), *De Civitate Dei Contra Paganos*, Heinemann, London, 1957.

Bachelder, Robert, 'The Gospel of Equality and the Gospel of Efficiency', www.religion-online.org.

Backhouse, Roger, E., *The Penguin History of Economics*, Princeton University Press, Penguin Books Ltd, 2002.

Bakunin, Jack, 'The Failure of Individualism', www.religion-online.org.

Beyer, Peter, *Religion and Globalisation*, Sage Publications, London, 1994.

Blamires, Harry, *The Christian Mind*, SPCK, London, 1963.

Blank, Rebecca M., *Is the Market Moral?* Brookings Institution Press, Washington, DC, 2004.

Bloom, Alan, *The Closing of the American Mind: How Higher Education has Failed Democracy and Impoverished the Soul's of Today's Students*, Penguin Books, New York, 1987.

Brueggemann, Walter, 'The Liturgy of Abundance, the Myth of Scarcity', www.religion-online.org.

Brunner, Emil, *Justice and the Social Order*, Butterworth, London, 1945.

Buber, Martin, *Between Man and Man*, Routledge & Kegan Paul, London, 1947.

Bush, Lawrence & Jeffrey Dekro, 'Sustainability and Shavuot', www.social action.com.

— 'Jews, Money, and Social Responsibility', www.questia.com.

Campbell, Deborah, 'What Economics Students in Three Countries are Doing to Put their Professors on the Defensive', www.paecon.net.

Capp, Walter H., 'Interpreting Vaclav Havel', www.aril.org.

Clark, Neil, 'How We Forgot the Art of Loving', *New Statesman*, 14th February, 2005.

Cobb, John B. Jr, 'Economics for the Common Good', www.religion-online.org.

— 'Economics as Idolatry', www.religion-online.org.

Charles, Rodger SJ, *Christian Social Witness and Teaching: The Catholic Tradition from Genesis to Centesimus Annus* (2 vols), Gracewing, Leominster, 1998.

Coleman, John A., 'Togetherness is All: In the Search of Justice', *Commonweal*, September, 1999.

Costa, John, D., *The Ethical Imperative: Why Moral Leadership is Good Business*, HarperCollins, Toronto, 1998.

Dalai Lama, His Holiness the (ed Sander Tideman), *Compassion or Competition: A Discussion of Human Values in Economics and Business*, Spirit in Business, Inc, Greenfield, MA, 2002.

Daly, Herman E. & John B. Cobb Jr, *For the Common Good*, Beacon Press, Boston, 1994.

Davis, Henry SJ, *Moral and Pastoral Theology* (Vol 1), Sheed & Ward, London & New York, 1949.

Dawson, Christopher (ed and annotated by Peter Milward, SJ), *The Rise of World Civilisation*, Kenkyusha, Tokyo, 1989.

De Santa Ana, Julio, 'Theological and Ethical Issues in the Age of Globalisation', www.cwmnote.com.

De Souza, Raymond J., 'Economics and Theology: A Wondrous Exchange', *Religion & Liberty*, May & June, 2001.

Duchrow, Ulrich, *Alternative to Global Capitalism: Drawn from Biblical History, Designed for Political Action*, International Books with Kairos Europa, Uttrecht, The Netherlands, 1998.

Ebenstien, Alan, 'The Poverty of Samuelson's Economics', www.freedom keys.com.

Economist, 'The Puzzling Failure of Economics', 23rd August, 1997.

Ely, Richard T., *Social Aspects of Christianity and Other Essays*, Thomas Y. Crowell, New York, 1889.

Frey, Donald E., 'The Good Samaritan as Bad Economist', www.aril.org.

Frey, Bruno & Alois Stutzer, *Happiness and Economics: How the Economy and Institutions Affect Well-being*, Princeton Universty Press, Princeton, 2001.

Fromm, Erich, *The Fear of Freedom*, Routledge & Kegan Paul, London, 1942.

— *The Sane Society*, Routledge & Kegan Paul, London, 1956.

— *The Art of Loving*, Thorsons, London, 1957.

Fullbrooke, Edward (ed), *A Guide to What's Wrong with Economics*, Anthem Press, London, 2004.

Gaffney, Mason & Fred Harrison, *The Corruption of Economics*, Shepheard-Walwyn, London, 1994.

Gold, Lorna, *The Sharing Economy: Solidarity Networks Transforming Globalisation*, Ashgate, Aldershot, 2004.

Goleman, Daniel (ed), *Healing Emotions*, Shambhala Publications, Boston, MA, 1997.

— *Emotional Intelligence*, Bantam Books, New York, 1999.

Graham, W. Fred, 'America's Other Religion', www.religion-online.org.

Greider, William, 'Beyond Scarcity: A New Story for American Capitalism', www.business-ethics.com.

Griffiths, Brian, *Morality and the Market Place: Christian Alternatives to Capitalism and Socialism*, Hodder & Stoughton, London, 1982.

Griffiths, Peter, *The Economist's Tale: A Consultant Encounters Hunger and the World Bank*, Zed Books, London, 2003.

Gurrien, Bernard, 'A Science Too Human? Economics', www.paecon.net.

Henderson, Hazel, *Beyond Globalization: Shaping a Sustainable Global Economy*, Kumarion Press, Bloomfield, CT, 1999.

Hutton, Will, 'Capitalism Must Put its House in Order', *The Observer*, 24th November, 2002.

'Ibn Khaldun', www.ummah.net.

John Paul II, *Centesimus Annus*, Daughters of St Paul, New York, 1991.

Keen, Steve, *Debunking Economics: The Naked Emperor of the Social Sciences*, Pluto Press, Annandale, NSW, 2001.

Kennedy, Carol, *Business Pioneers: How Three Families became Household Names, Sainsbury, John Lewis, Cadbury*, Random House, London, 2000.

Keynes, J.M., *Essays in Persuasion*, Harcourt, Brace & Co, New York, 1932.

Kuran, Timur, 'The Genesis of Islamic Economics: A Chapter in the Politics of Muslim Identity', *Social Research*, Summer 1997.

Land, Philip, SJ, *Catholic Social Teaching as I Have Lived, Loathed and Loved It*, Loyola University Press, Chicago, 1994.

Landes, David, *The Wealth and Poverty of Nations*, Little Brown & Co, New York, 1998.

Leibniz, G.W. (trans E.M. Huggard, ed Austin Farrar), *Theodicy: Essays on the Goodness of God, the Freedom of Man and the Origin of Evil*, Routledge, London, 1951 [1710].

Long, D. Stephen, *Divine Economy: Theology and the Market*, Routledge, London & New York, 2000.

— 'Bernard Dempsey's Theological Economics: Usury, Profit, and Human Fulfilment', www.questia.com.

Lutz, Mark A., *Economics for the Common Good: Two Centuries of Social Economic Thought in the Humanistic Tradition*, Routledge, London & New York, 1999.

Maclaurin, Colin, *An Account of Sir Isaac Newton's Philosophical Discoveries*, Nourse, London, 3rd edn, 1775.

Makewell, Raymond (ed), *Economic Wisdom*, New Frontier, Epping, NSW, 2001.

Marshall, A., *Principles of Economics*, Macmillan & Co, London, 1930.

Martin, Jacques, 'The Death of Intimacy: A Selfish, Market-driven Society is Eroding our Very Humanity', *The Guardian*, Saturday 18th September, 2004.

Moe-Lobeda, Cynthia D., *Healing a Broken World: Globalisation and God*, Fortress Press, Minneapolis, 2002.

Mofid, Kamran, *Globalisation for the Common Good*, Shepheard-Walwyn, London, 2002.

— *Business Ethics, Corporate Social Responsibility and Globalisation for the Common Good*, Shepherd-Walwyn, London, 2003.

Nahj al-Balaghah, 'Sermons of the Commander of the Faithful', Imam Ali b. Abi Talib, www.al-islam.org.

Nemetz, A., 'Common Good', *The New Catholic Encyclopaedia*, McGraw Hill, New York, 1966.

Newbigin, Leslie, *Foolishness to the Greeks: The Gospel and Western Culture*, Eerdmans, Michigan, 1986.

Neuhaus, Father Richard John, 'The Secularism of the West', www.catholic education.org.

Newman, John Henry (ed Ian Ker), *The Idea of a University*, Clarendon, Oxford, 1976 [1873].

Niebuhr, Reinhold, *Moral Man and Immoral Society*, Scibners, New York, 1932.

North, Douglass C., *Institutions, Institutional Change and Economic Performance*, Cambridge University Press, 1990.

'Open Letter from Economic Students to Professors and Others Responsible for the Teaching of this Discipline', Student Petition of Autisme-Economie, www.paecon.net.

Orlean, Andre, 'Humility in Economics', www.paecon.net.

Ormerod, Paul, *The Death of Economics*, Faber & Faber, London, 1994.

— *Butterfly Economics*, Faber & Faber, London, 1998.

Oslington, Paul, 'A Theological Economics', www.case.edu.au.

— 'Christian Theology and Economics: A Reading Guide', www.zadok.org.au.

Oweiss, Ibrahim M., 'Ibn-Khaldun: The Father of Economics', www.george town.edu.

Patience, Allan, 'Is There a Theology of Globalisation? Responding to David Batstone', *Zadok Perspective*, Winter 1999.

Post, Stephen G., 'Unlimited Love: What It Is and Why It Matters', www. unlimitedloveinstitute.org.

Post-autistic Economic Review, www.paecon.net, selected issues.

Pourafzal, Haleh & Roger Montgomery, *The Spiritual Wisdom of Hafez: Teachings of the Philosopher of Love*, Inner Traditions, Rochester, 1998.

Raiser, Konrad, *For a Culture of Life: Transforming Globalisation and Violence*, WCC Publications, Geneva, 2002.

Riley, Robert, 'The Intersection of Theology and Economics: Is it the Empty Set?', www.stthomas.edu.

Ranson, D., *The No Nonsense Guide to Fair Trade*, Verso, London, 2001.

Rawls, J., *A Theory of Justice*, Harvard University Press, Cambridge, Mass, 1971.

Rowbotham, Michael, *The Grip of Death: A Study of Mondern Money, Debt Slavery and Destructive Economics*, John Carpenter Publishing, Charlbury, Oxon, 1998.

— Sen, Amartya, *Development as Freedom*, Alfred Knopf, New York, 1999.

Roze, Janis, 'Opening the Door to a New Humanity', www.kosmosjournal.org.

Sacks, Rabbi Jonathan, 'Judaism's Religious Vision and the Capitalist Ethic', *Religion & Liberty*, November & December, 2001.

Samuelson, Paul, *Foundations of Economic Analysis*, Harvard University Press, Cambridge, Mass, 1948.

Schumacher, E.F., *Small is Beautiful: Economics as if People Mattered*, Bland & Briggs, London, 1973.

— *A Guide for the Perplexed*, Jonathan Cape, London, 1977.

Sen, Amartya, *On Ethics and Economics*, Basil Blackwell, Oxford, 1998.

Senge, Peter, *The Fifth Discipline*, Random House, London, 1990.

Shinn, Roger, 'Christian Faith and Economic Practice', at www.christiancentury. org.

Smith, Adam, *An Inquiry Into the Nature and Causes of Wealth of Nations*, Kathryn Sutherland (ed), Oxford University Press, Oxford, revised edn, 1998.

Soros, George, *Open Society: Reforming Global Capitalism*, BBS Public Affairs, New York, 2000.

Stanford, Jim, 'Confessions of a Recovering Economist', www.paecon.net.

Stebbins, J. Michael, 'Business, Faith and the Common Good', *Review of Business*, Fall, 1997.

Stott, John R.W., *Issues Facing Christians Today*, Marshalls, London, 1983.

Tamari, Meir, 'Wealth, Torah, and Morality', www.questia.com.

— 'Public Morality: The Jewish Contribution', *Religion & Liberty*, November & December, 1993.

Taskhiri, Ayatullah Muhammad Ali, 'Islamic Economy: Its Ideological and Legal Foundations', www.al-islam.org.

Tawney, R.H., *The Acquisitive Society*, G. Bell & Sons, London, 1921.

— *Religion and the Rise of Capitalism*, John Murray, London, 1926.

— *Equality*, George Allen & Unwin, London, 1931.

Temple, William, *Christianity and Social Order*, Shepheard-Walwyn, London, 1976.

Tideman, Sander G., 'Towards a New Paradigm in Economics and Development', www.spiritinbusiness.org.

Titmuss, Richard (trans Talcott Parsons), *The Gift Relationship*, George, Allen & Unwin, London, 1970.

Tomer, John F., 'Human Well-being: A New Approach Based on Overall and Ordinary Functionings', www.questia.com.

Umer Chapra, M., 'Islamic Economics Offer the Best to Mankind', www. islamicvoice.com.

Velasquez, Manuel, *et al*, 'The Common Good', www.scu.edu.

Waterman, A.M.C., 'Economics as Theology: Adam Smith's *Wealth of Nations*', www.questia.com.

Weber, M., *The Protestant Ethic and the Spirit of Capitalism*, Scribners, New York, 1958.

Welch, Patrick J. & J.J. Mueller, 'The Relationships of Religion to Economics', www.questia.com.

Wilson, Rodney, 'Comparative Religious Thought on Economics Behaviour and Financial Transactions', www.questia.com.

Wuthnow, Robert, 'Religion and Economic Life', in N. Smelser & R. Swedberg, *The Handbook of Economic Sociology*, Princeton University Press, Princeton, 1994.

www.ummah.net, 'A Note on Ibn-Khaldun'.

Young, John, *The Natural Economy*, Shepeard-Walwyn, London, 1996.

Yuengert, Andrew M., 'The Common Good for Economists', *Faith & Economics*, Number 38, Fall, 2001.

Yunus, Muhammad, with Alan Jolis, *Banker to the Poor*, Aurum Press, London, 1999.

Zinbarg, Edward, *Faith, Morals and Money: What the World's Religions Tell Us about Money in the Marketplace*, The Continuum Publishing Group Ltd, New York & London, 2001.

Epilogue

BY BHAI SAHIB MOHINDER SINGH

I AM BOTH humbled and honoured to be asked to write an epilogue to this book by Kamran Mofid and Marcus Braybrooke. I first met Kamran three years ago when he was organising his first International Conference on an Interfaith Perspective on Globalisation for the Common Good in Oxford. It was encouraging to hear an economist say that modern economics had lost its way and that, to find its way back, it needed the help of religion. He had the breadth and wisdom to recognise that, in a global economy, religion would have to draw on the insights of all great faiths. I have much enjoyed our debate and dialogue on the relevance and significance of theological economics in this age of globalisation.

I have also been much blessed by knowing the Reverend Marcus Braybrooke, a leading international figure in interfaith dialogue. As we prepare for the fourth Conference at Kericho in Kenya, it is my pleasure to endorse the contributions of both authors and to say something of the Sikh point of view.

In their eloquent submission, they have positively demonstrated how, by sharing the wisdom and inspiration that emanates from all great faiths, religions can and should foster the justice and peace which will lead to the realisation of Globalisation for the Common Good.

The Sikh faith is a monotheistic religion which emphasises social and gender equality whilst stressing the importance of living in God's presence at all times, working hard with total honesty, being generous to the less fortunate and generally serving others.

The Sikh religion began in India, in the Punjab, 536 years ago with the coming into this world of Guru Nanak Dev Ji in 1469. Guru Nanak, the first Prophet of the Sikh faith, was followed successively by nine other mortal Prophets, until the last Guru, Guru Gobind Singh Ji, left for the heavenly abode in 1708. Before his departure, he ordained the faith's sacred text to be the Sikhs' perpetual Guru for all time to come.

The Sikh Scripture tells us that there dwell on this globe 8.4 million species of life on the land, in the water and in the atmosphere, each playing its role in the divine plan. All species carry within them a spark of life which one may consider part of the infinite Divine Flame, or the Creator. All life forms on this earthly globe also fit into a spiritual scale ascending from pure matter to pure spirit. Pure matter, at the lower end, is followed by the vegetable kingdom, the animal kingdom and the human kingdom; pure spirit is at the top: it is what we refer to as God.

Mankind is the most evolved species – it is within the human kingdom that beings are blessed with reason. They are bequeathed the kingship of the universe and are responsible for its protection and well-being. This unique power of reasoning is bestowed upon humans for differentiating between good and evil. Evil and good have always coexisted and will continue to do so: these opposites are necessary for the progression of the soul. We are not judged until the end of our lives, to enable us to exercise choice and decide which path to follow. The Sikh religious tradition is based on profound love and humility. If one cannot show an abundance of love for God's creation, one will never be able to love God.

It is stated in this book that 'spiritual revolution needs architecture and dedicated architects'. Let the foundation be love, humility, mercy, compassion, truthfulness and forgiveness. This is the foundation of any religion. If you take these things away, the religion will collapse. Forgiveness, especially, cannot be forsaken even for a moment, no matter what the odds. A merciful person is concerned and lives for the welfare of others, hating the sin not the sinner.

In the Sikh holy Scripture the Muslim Saint Farid proclaims that we are morally required to do good even to the wicked, and not to seek revenge. The Sikh faith requires the aggrieved to venture even further, going to the oppressor to seek forgiveness. Retaliation and revenge are futile. As we are constantly asking the Lord for love, mercy, compassion and forgiveness, we should exercise the same love, mercy, compassion and forgiveness ourselves.

Furthermore, the Sikh faith has an exemplary tradition of selflessness, or *nishkaamta*, which requires one not only to respect all the religions of the world, but also to sacrifice oneself for others if need be. This was practically demonstrated by Guru Tegh Bahadur Ji, the ninth Prophet of the Sikh faith, who laid down his life for Hinduism. Nobody else has sacrificed himself for another faith in this way. Guru Gobind Singh Ji states that we must recognise the whole of humanity as one family. The Sikhs will fight for any just cause, it does not matter whose cause it is. A Christian once said, 'Sikhs are created as a gift to humanity.' They were ordained to be *'Akaal Purakh ki Fauj'* by Guru Gobind Singh Ji: God's army, ready to sacrifice themselves for the good of humanity.

In the Sikh sacred text, Guru Granth Sahib Ji begins by asserting, *'Ik Onkar'*: there is only one God. He was present before time, He is very much present now and will be for all time to come. The fact that all of us have only one Heavenly Father, who is also our Heavenly Mother, Brother, Sister and Protector, unites us all within the global family of faiths. With a common spiritual parentage, logic demands that we perceive of all humanity as brothers and sisters. Diverse as we may be, we each belong to each other and to God, and He belongs to us all. He is our common denominator.

The Sikh faith lifts boundaries and offers a constructive model for the practical application of interfaith work. This is evident through its sacred Scripture, its history and its living traditions. Guru Nanak travelled far and wide to have dialogue with other faith leaders. He encouraged Hindus to become better Hindus and Muslims to become better Muslims. His lifelong companions were a Muslim musician, Bhai Mardana, and a Hindu, Bhai Bala. The fifth Guru, Guru Arjan Dev Ji, asked Sai Mian Mir, a Muslim Saint, to lay the foundation stone of the Harmandir Sahib, and the divine writings of Hindu, Muslim and Sikh Saints are contained within the holy Scripture, whose divine message is exalted to the position of perpetual Guru, or Prophet.

The Sikh tradition of *Langar* is also a fine example of interfaith principle and co-operation. It is a practical manifestation of equality, where all are made welcome and required to sit on the same level, irrespective of caste, gender, creed and social or religious status. *Langar* is also an opportunity for strangers to feed strangers, and in doing so to realise that there really are no strangers in the House of God. This free kitchen tradition was the highlight at the fourth global Interfaith Parliament of the World's Religions held in Barcelona in July 2004. Over seven thousand participants of different faiths were served daily. In Barcelona, *Langar* became the Sikh's 'simple but profound act'. People were touched by the exuberant spirit of selfless giving. Its practical manifestation of equality and inter-dependence left an indelible mark.

The need for such interfaith initiatives is paramount, as the twenty-first century poses new challenges for human-ity. There are challenges of division. Alliances at all levels of society based on politics, race, economic and military groupings, tend to serve vested interests and cause global segregation instead of desperately needed unification.

Globalisation, spurred on by the communications revo-lution, has thrown the peoples of the world closer together. In theory it has removed man-made borders – which faiths have tried to break down for a long time. There is a vast exchange of information, and of people, which has brought its own challenges. The movement of people creates refugees and problems concerning development. There are heightened security issues and greater media responsibilities. States that once covertly repressed populations in isolation can no longer do so. The media drive the information revolution, but also need to be a positive influence for the common good. This is another challenge. Technology could strangle humanity: we must control it, not be enslaved by it.

Globalisation has also brought the challenge of new forms of conflict and violence. A social, cultural and institutional 'fault line' has developed and the world seems to have lost its equilibrium. Terrorism is now more sophisticated and better organised. The terrorist has become invisible, threatening the concept of borders. 9/11, and the Bali and Madrid suicide bombings, arise from the human failings of ignorance, doubt, suspicion and lack of understanding. And retaliatory action does not resolve the real terrorism which plagues remote villages across the globe with the constant threat of potential death and destruction. Over thirty thousand people die from the lack of basic food and water every day in this new millennium!

'Economic globalisation' – or we can say 'global exploitation' – is on the increase. An elite minority has found a new and more lethal tool for the accelerated economic exploitation of the globe and the majority of its inhabitants. From the Sikh spiritual perspective, exploitative globalisation is immoral and unethical, causing misery for the marginalised; it is against the laws of nature, and against the heavenly Father's divine plan. Ironically, it destroys not only those it exploits but also, ultimately, those who practise this exploitation under the guise of economic necessity.

Humanity is at a crossroads: we need to choose between globalisation for the common good and globalisation for the individual good. Recent tragedies have touched souls. Globalisation, through technology and commerce, is

taking a firmer hold but there is an unprecedented opportunity for 'faith' to elevate and illuminate the human mind,
to engender peace and harmony on our planet. Humanity
should stand up to this challenge, take spirituality seriously
and use it for the common good – or suffer the consequences of human greed, exploitation and arrogance.

The current state of the world is described in this book
as a 'bitter harvest'. The Sikh Scripture tells of 'a famine of
Truth, and endemic falsehood'. The only remedy is spiritual regeneration. Unless we charge ourselves spiritually, we
will not be able to face the challenges of this world.
Humanity cannot divorce itself from spirituality, just as the
mortal body cannot divorce itself from the spirit, or soul.
The negation of religion is the negation of the existence of
God, and of one's soul. We may fail to appreciate and
understand our spirit but it would be folly to say that it
doesn't exist. Without the presence of a spirit within us,
we would all be corpses. Any human endeavour is hollow
and exploitative unless in contains a spiritual or ethical
dimension.

If we are mesmerized by science and its technological
advances, and become more and more science-centred
rather than spirit-centred, we will be inviting destruction.
Religion and science are humanity's two indispensable
knowledge systems. They are often seen to be in conflict
but, when they team up to work in harmony for the benefit of humanity, they have an overwhelming impact and are
an awesome combination. The basic principle behind each
is the same: the search for 'truth'. Science seeks truth in
the physical, secular world and has brought us many material comforts. Religion searches the inner realm of the
human spirit to establish a link with its divine origin and
achieve inner contentment. 'Within the mind dwell untold
jewels, gems and rubies of spiritual knowledge, waiting to
be discovered.'

As long as scientific 'advance' is guided by spiritual wisdom there is the hope of generating enormous prosperity

for the good of all. In the twenty-first century humanity faces the enormous challenge of fusing the two in a positive way. The vast spiritual treasures in the Scriptures await humanity – to utilise and capitalise upon. Armed with them, we can face modern challenges. The Scriptures teach us to be kind, forgiving, compassionate, truthful, unselfish, humble and loving – all of these being the ingredients which we need for the non-exploitative development of the globe.

Good values are godly values and these have to be defended at all cost if humanity is not to be at risk. Guru Nanak teaches us that, unless an individual has inner peace, he cannot generate external peace. Without moral values all will be lost. Morality is fine, but the practical application of morality should override the theory of morality. Guru Nanak's message is a commandment which humanity should take seriously: 'Higher than truth is truthful conduct.'

The Sikh tradition requires one to be a worldly being, not a recluse or hermit. Man must earn his living through the sweat of his brow, and serve himself and others whilst remembering God. Guru Nanak taught three basic tenets: *naam japo*, *kirat karo*, and *wand shako*: pray and be in communion with God at all times; work hard and honestly and be conscious at all times of God's presence; and share generously with others what you have. To attain 'spiritual wealth', after which all else will follow, one must lead a life imbued with *simran* (meditation) and *sewa* (selfless service) – not for one's own benefit but for *sarbat ka bhalla* (the welfare for all).

One example of this is in the community co-operative Marag Sat Santokh Manufacturers Ltd (MSS) of Birmingham, England, set up in 1980 by the founder Saints of Guru Nanak Nishkam Sewak Jatha. While providing employment, MSS also addresses the issues of social and economic regeneration. The emphasis is on service as opposed to profit, and there is a strong faith element.

Members of Sikh society have a dual duty: to their physical livelihood and to their souls. Honest service for the improvement of the community can be done with *tan* (the body, or manual service), *dhan* (money, or material service) and *man* (mind, or intellectual service.) For a Sikh, his workplace should also be his place of worship. Work is combined with spirituality: the notion is that 'work is worship'. Our Scripture tells us that, 'Those who trade in the Lord's Name are wealthy.' When spirituality is incorporated into secular trading, the latter is blessed.

In its opening chapter, *Japji Sahib*, the Sikh Scripture reminds us that the globe we inhabit as spiritual refugees is really intended by God to be a *dharmsaal*, a gigantic place of worship. God established this planet as a sort of faith school in which we must sow the seeds of spirituality and live with responsibility towards God's creation. In this spirit we should encourage partnerships between the family of world faiths to address the collective future of humanity and to treat the planet as sacred. Globalisation for the common good is a noble initiative requiring forgiveness, compassion, truthfulness, humility, charity and love for all men – in fact respect for God's entire creation. Man made in the image of God must emulate His qualities – he must love and respect the Creator's Creation.

Finally, as both Kamran and the Reverend Braybrooke have proposed – and I wish to endorse their recommendations – economics and theology should be made to work together for the common good. The vitality of a society is not just a matter of economics and trade, but also of religion. The religious impulse unifies a society and culture. A society which has lost its religion and its spirituality becomes a society which has lost its culture. Sooner or later it will fail to exist, as did many civilisations before it.

The ethical and spiritual teachings of all religions, and their striving for the common good, can provide a clear and focused model of moral behaviour in what has been termed 'the marketplace'. Religious concepts such as human dignity, communal solidarity, humility, patience, service, compassion, reciprocity and social justice should go together with business values such as equity, efficiency, growth and profit to give us globalisation for the common good, in which everyone gains. We should indeed acknowledge that the marketplace is not just an economic sphere, 'it is a region of the human spirit', of compassion and dignity.

I also agree that, in order to carry out our task for the common good most effectively and efficiently, we should establish a proper home for it – The Centre for the Study of Globalisation for the Common Good. We will earnestly endeavour to help Kamran and all those who have joined him to continue the journey, which we began together in Oxford in 2002, to connect people from all over the world in the interests of the common good; to attempt, with compassion and justice, to find solutions; to heal our fractured world; and to balance the world of business, commerce and trade with spirituality, nature and society.

We are today all global citizens, part of a global community. In economic terms, we have moved beyond Gross Domestic Product: the issues confronting us now are those of 'Gross Global Product'. God has bequeathed to humanity natural global resources which do not belong to individuals or single communities, and humanity must learn to share them. There is at present an imbalance between the 'developed world' and the 'developing world'. The 'superpowers', though a minority, hold most of the the monetary assets and command the power of technology. The developing countries are poor even though they have an abundance of human and natural resources. Morality demands that there is fair trading and reciprocal respect. Resources should be made fluid and should be exchanged in such a way as to create a world of parity, producing a Gross Global Product in which future generations can invest.

Globalisation for the Common Good

Kamran Mofid

'This book is devastating in its exposure of the failures of the present structures of our national and global economic systems … a good and highly readable book on an important theme. We need more of these tracts for our times, and the fleshing out of alternative strategies. Millions of lives depend on it'

John Gladwin, Bishop of Guildford in CHURCH TIMES

'… a visionary and humane critique of globalisation that merits broad and urgent attention. As an economist, he writes with particular conviction of the need to leaven an interests- and profits-based science of economics with considerations of justice and the common good'

James Piscatori, Professor of Islam and International Relations, Oxford

'… a helpful and readable contribution to the whole debate about globalisation. This challenges the view that "there is no alternative" and helps us think about what that alternative might look like'

Christine Allen, Catholic Institute for International Relations, London

'… a remarkable book … the most penetrating analysis I have read on this topic, as well as the proposal that is the most optimistic'

Stanley Krippner, Professor of Psychology, Saybrook Graduate School, San Francisco

'Kamran Mofid's book raises important questions about the way students are taught and is a critical challenge to the profound assumptions which allow the separation of academic study and spirituality from the injustices of our world which urgently needs to be remedied'

Christopher Rowland, Dean Ireland's Professor of Exegesis of Holy Scripture, Queen's College, Oxford

'Without any doubt, this book marks a turning point in the debate on what type of economic education we need to receive in the new age … This book is enormously stimulating, provocative and enriching'

Professor Hooshang Amirahmadi, Director, Middle East Centre, Rutgers University

128pp   ISBN 0 85683 195 6   £10.95 pb

Business Ethics, Corporate Social Responsibility and Globalisation for the Common Good

Kamran Mofid

Economic justice for the whole world is the key to solving many of our social and political problems. For economic answers we must return to the classical economists, but with a global, multi-faith perspective.

This short study is an appeal to the deep, instinctive understanding of the common good which all people share. It is an appeal to our essential humanity. It deals with some of the most pressing concerns of people the world over, concerns which every generation must consider and answer. It is written in the hope of inspiring idealism and a desire to give practical help.

44pp   ISBN 0 85683 217 0   £5.00

The Natural Economy

John Young

'A true grasp of how the economy should be constituted shows it to be a thing of harmony and beauty, all its parts cooperating for the common good, and its inbuilt laws distributing benefits equitably.'
John Young

The author argues that economics is fundamentally an ethical science for it is about an order that is natural to humanity. The implementation of a natural economic order will bring justice; its neglect will bring injustice.

'In its quiet and exact way it is more radically revolutionary than the works of Marx. It is more radical, because it goes more surely to the root of economics. It is also revolutionary, but far from advocating violence, the book begins its revolution by engendering understanding of what is wrong.'   **AD 2000**

'The treatment brings out that aspect which is most important to the understanding of matters economic, namely, that it signifies an abundance of goods or wealth for all. This is in stark contrast to the miserable modern vision of scarcity as the guiding principle of all economic thinking.'
CATHOLIC WEEKLY

160pp   ISBN 0 85683 166 2   £10.95 pb

Progress and Poverty

**An inquiry into the cause of industrial depressions
and the increase of want with the increase of wealth
... The Remedy**

Henry George

The important social issues raised in this classic of economic literature remain unresolved to this day. George's non-violent solution to poverty has been all but forgotten, although it had widespread support around the world and was endorsed by Churchill and four British Prime Ministers during the 20th century.

Full Edition   ISBN 0 91131 279 X   £24.95 hb
Full Edition   ISBN 0 91131 258 7   £14.95 pb
Abridged Edition   ISBN 0 91131 210 2   £9.95pb

From Wasteland to Promised Land

Robert V. Andelson & James M. Dawsey

Persons of good will search widely for realistic models of social transformation. In the wake of the failures of both socialist states and capitalist economies, the authors demonstrate how awareness of land as the basic source of human wealth can be developed to address the problem of poverty. The authors argue that misuse of land constitutes the root problem of human poverty and national underdevelopment. With clarity and insight this pioneering book cuts through the inadequacies of traditional solutions to the dilemmas of poverty. At a time when the alternatives often seem to be between selfish pursuit of wealth and ineffectual idealism, the authors retrieve a transcendent religious view of community that is realistic both about economics and about human nature.

'This is a book that will repay study… The authors must be commended for taking the question of poverty seriously and for the careful way they offer a solution'   **BAPTIST TIMES**

160pp   ISBN 0 85683 133 6   £10.95 pb